D1317003

TALKS IN A FREE COUNTRY

TALKS IN A
FREE COUNTRY

by

WILLIAM   RALPH   INGE

Essay Index Reprint Series

 BOOKS FOR LIBRARIES PRESS

FREEPORT, NEW YORK

LIBRARY
WAYNE STATE COLLEGE
WAYNE, NEBRASKA

First Published 1942
Reprinted 1972

Library of Congress Cataloging in Publication Data

Inge, William Ralph, 1860-1954.
   Talks in a free country.

   (Essay index reprint series)
   Reprint of the 1942 ed.
   I. Title.
AC8.I535 1972   824'.9'12   77-167365
ISBN 0-8369-2774-5

PRINTED IN THE UNITED STATES OF AMERICA
BY
NEW WORLD BOOK MANUFACTURING CO., INC.
HALLANDALE, FLORIDA 33009

PREFACE
(TO ORIGINAL EDITION)

Events are moving so fast that thoughts written down for the Press in August may be out of date in October. The fifth Act in a terrible world-tragedy is still to come, and the dénouement of the plot is hidden from us. The actors will not belong to my generation.

W. R. INGE

Brightwell Manor
August, 1942

202938

202538

"Materialism is the auxiliary doctrine of every tyranny. To crush the spiritual human man by specialising him; to create not human beings but wheels for the great social machine; to give them not conscience but society for a general principle; to enslave the soul to things; to depersonalise man, is the dominant tendency of our epoch. What is threatened is moral liberty, the very nobility of man."

Amiel.

"Der Weg der neueren Bildung geht
Von Humanität
Durch Nationalität
Zur Bestialität."

Grillparzer.

"Must a government of necessity be too strong for the liberties of its own people, or too weak to maintain its own existence?"

Abraham Lincoln.

"When a nation boils, the scum always rises to the top."

Lord Snell.

"Criminal means once tolerated are soon preferred. They present a shorter cut to the object than through the highway of the moral virtues. Justifying perfidy and murder for public benefit, public benefit would soon become the pretext, and perfidy and murder the end, until rapacity, revenge, and fear more dreadful than revenge, would satiate their insatiable appetites."

Burke.

"Ordo renascendi est crescere posse malis."

Rutilius.

CONTENTS

ESCAPE

SCENE: *Puddlecombe Abbas, Dorset, the house of Lord Winterbourne.*

SPEAKERS: *Lord Winterbourne, formerly a Governor in India; Perry, a retired Calcutta merchant; Pundit Bhagavan Chandra; Bishop Waldegrave.*

WINTERBOURNE   Welcome, Perry, to your last visit at Puddlecombe.

PERRY   My last visit? Don't you want to see me again?

WINTERBOURNE   The military have taken over my house; I have to clear out next week. But I could not live here anyhow. No money and no servants.

PERRY   Shall you not be very sorry to go?

WINTERBOURNE   Very sorry indeed. All the time I was in India I dreamed of spending my old age here. I remembered the velvety green lawns, the lime avenue, the panelled hall with the portraits by Raeburn of my great-grandparents, and the little church with its old tower. But now all is over. Not only is my home gone, but my family. My only son was killed in 1918; and now his son—he was only married two years—is missing at Singapore. I shall never see him again. My brother died without children; my married sister lives in New Zealand; I never see my daughter-in-law. What have I to live for? Absolutely nothing.

PERRY   What do you mean to do, Winterbourne? You must do something and live somewhere.

WINTERBOURNE I have been doing a little Home Guard work, but that ends when I leave this house. I want to go into a hermitage, "the world forgetting, by the world forgot". It can only be for a few years. But honestly I want help and advice, and that is why I have asked three of my old friends in India to come and say good-bye to poor old Puddlecombe with me. You know, when I was in India, I tried to study Indian philosophy, and was rather drawn to that way of life. So I have asked my old friend Chandra; he is in England on some government job. He will represent Hindu philosophy; and Bishop Waldegrave, who has given up his diocese in India, will represent the Church of England. And you, old chap, what do you represent?

PERRY Oil, a useful lubricant; and the affection of an old friend. But my dear Winterbourne, I don't want you to chuck everything. You are not past work, though I am.

WINTERBOURNE I don't want to chuck everything, though there is precious little left for me to chuck. But I want to be able to escape in thought from the ruins of my world, and that is what Hinduism and Christianity, in their different ways, promise to provide—a refuge from the slings and arrows of outrageous fortune.

PERRY It seems to me that most people are trying to escape from themselves, if not from the world. I travelled down in the same compartment with a middle-aged man who was doing crossword puzzles; a woman who was reading the *Daily Mirror* straight through; a boy with a detective novel; and two girls who jabbered to each other about nothing at all, the whole way to Templecombe. It is rather odd that though we look forward to an eternity of calm fruition, we cannot spend an hour without trying to escape from a gentleman whom we know slightly and find, it seems, an intolerable bore—ourself.

WINTERBOURNE Boredom is a mild form of unhappiness. But I think its effects in history are underestimated. The French were bored with Louis Philippe because he governed them prosaically, and they sacked him, putting Napoleon the Little in his place. Determined not to repeat the mistake, Louis Napoleon gave them "glory", of which the stages were the Crimea, Solferino, Mexico, and Sedan. Boredom would soon bring to an end all the static Utopias, and the farmyard socialism of the Fabians. Boredom generates wars, which are not boring. The criminals who arrange them have studied the minds of the masses who vote for them, and of the young men who gallantly die in them. Boredom, however, is not my trouble at all. Crossword puzzles are of no use to me.

PERRY I ought not to have introduced the subject; it is really irrelevant. Unhappiness, not boredom, makes people wish to escape in imagination into a happier time or a happier place. This may be in the past or in the future. Your other guests will not talk about escape into the past; but for my own part when I wished to escape from the sordid cares of business I used to immerse myself in history. This dream-world in the past is, I suppose, the cradle of romanticism. It has often been a very popular resort. "The old is better." "Our forefathers had more wit and wisdom than we." There was once a golden age, the kingdom of Saturn, when the earth was kindly and men were virtuous. At the back of men's minds was the thought that since there was once a golden age there may and probably will be another. The "sorrowful weary wheel" may "go back and fetch the age of gold". In any case, nothing can rob us of the happiness which we once enjoyed,* and oddly enough we can take pleasure in the thought of the happiness of antiquity, and of posterity.

WINTERBOURNE The misunderstood doctrine of evolution and the myth of human perfectibility have made our contemporaries despise the past. But you are quite right; reverence for antiquity as such has played an important part in history. Respect for authority has made religion, for good and evil, the most powerful of antiseptics. And there is a curious charm about anything old, for some people at any rate. Horace Walpole says, " I almost think there is no wisdom comparable to that of exchanging what are called the realities of life for dreams. Old castles, old pictures, old histories, and the babble of old people, make one live back into centuries which cannot disappoint one. The dead have exhausted their power of deceiving."

PERRY And the result—Strawberry Hill Gothic!

WINTERBOURNE Which things are an allegory. Archaists are not only dreamers; they try to revive what never existed except in their imaginations. In a disintegrating society men despise the recent past, and try to restore something more primitive. In the arts, including architecture, this has happened more than once. We have lost nearly the whole of Greek literature after Aristotle, because the Attic revival disliked the style in which it was written. And we at home have had our church restorers and our primitivist painters and sculptors. In your reading of history, have you

* "Nostrum est quod praeteriit temporis." *Seneca.*

not noticed the ghosts which hover disastrously over the modern world—the dream of a universal church, of a new Roman empire, of conquering Vikings, and so forth? How else can we account for Mussolini and Hitler? Perverted romanticism is always obscene and sadistic, almost insane.

PERRY   Yes, you won't be tempted to escape in that direction. But there is much in history which is consoling as well as much that is discouraging. There have been flowering times of civilisation in which it is good to live in thought. Their creations of wisdom and beauty don't perish; they are treasures for ever.

WINTERBOURNE   I don't forget that my favourite books were written long ago. But the best literature and art are not archaic; they are timeless. Still, I am glad we have had a short discussion of archaism as an escape, for we shall not hear much of that this afternoon. I think I hear the car which is bringing the Bishop and the Pundit from the station. My idea is that we should lunch together and then adjourn to the summer-house which is a favourite seat of mine. I shall then ask the Indian to preach us a sermon for my benefit, after which the Bishop, who is not at all a conventional parson, will give us his views. I have hopes that between them they will help me to grapple with the extreme despondency which I now feel. I think it is partly being turned out of my family home that makes me realise that I have lived too long. At present I wish I was in my "underground shelter".

PERRY   I shall not be sorry when I hear that my number is up. The world belongs to the young, and a nice mess they seem likely to make of it. Here are your other guests.

* * * *

WINTERBOURNE Well, Chandra, you got my letter, and you know why I want your help. If you will be so good, I should like you to explain to us what you believe about our position and duties in the world. I know, when one asks an educated Indian what his religion has done for him, he usually answers, "Escape" or "Deliverance". Well, we Westerners used to say that we did not want to escape. The world may not be the best of all possible worlds, but it is a pleasant enough place to live in, and always interesting. "A man who has found his work, and who is happily married, has squared his accounts with life." So said Hegel, and so said Carlyle. But now we are on our beam ends; our world is falling into ruins; and we are beginning to suspect that our optimistic philosophy was rather shallow. "There is a way that seemeth right unto a man," says the Book of Proverbs; "but the end thereof are the ways of death." Carlyle's gospel of work is not enough. We are beginning to ask, as Clough tells us not to do, "Go, say not in thine heart, And what then, were it accomplished, were the wild impulse allayed, what were the use and the good?" I believe you in India look on our restless activities, as Matthew Arnold says, "with patient deep disdain". We are no longer too proud to listen; we are off the track, somehow. At any rate I want to escape from Europe in 1942. Whoever wins this war will find it a tough job to win the peace. I am an old man and can do nothing, except by remembering the old Greek proverb, "The deeds of the young, the counsels of the middle-aged, and the prayers of the old".

CHANDRA When Kipling says that East is East and West is West, and never the two shall meet, he simplifies too much. There is not much that I am going to say that you will not find in the Gospels, but, if the Bishop will forgive me, the West has understood Christ no better than China has understood Gautama. And there is very little that you will not find in Plato. But Plato was a Pythagorean, and we Indians believe that Pythagoras was not a Greek at all, but a Hindu. His name is lost, but his affectionate disciples called him Pitta Guru, "Father Teacher".

WINTERBOURNE Go and tell them that at Oxford, Chandra.

CHANDRA And Plotinus, at the risk of his life, set out for India to learn the wisdom of the Brahmins.

WINTERBOURNE But he never got there.

CHANDRA The name of "Boutta" was familiar at Alexandria. I could prove to you that some Indian thinkers are Western in type and that many Western mystics have been in full sympathy with India. Even the Jews sometimes wished they had the wings of a dove. Even Sophocles thought that the best fate is not to be born. Your Bacon repeats this sentiment. And what of Schopenhauer, who tells us to renounce the will to live? And "patient deep disdain" has not been exactly the reaction of one Far Eastern Power to Europeanism at its worst; you are learning that to your cost. However, I have promised to tell you, as briefly as I can, what I believe. I think it is fairly typical of my countrymen. I must however insist that to speak of Indian thought is almost as misleading as to speak of English or German thought. For instance, no Indian writer is so well known in Europe as Rabindranath Tagore. As a poet, he is thoroughly Indian; as a thinker, he is so far westernised that many of our philosophers refuse to regard him as representative. He thinks that we in India have carried detachment too far; he holds that life has a value, and that action must not be disparaged. On the other side, Emerson, the American, carries his acceptance of the Indian doctrine of the unity of all life so far that he has lent himself to caricature. Oh yes! I know Andrew Lang's parody:

> "I am the batsman and the bat;
> I am the bowler and the ball;
> The umpire, the pavilion cat,
> The roller, pitch, and stumps and all."

And even in purely Indian philosophy and religion there are many differences. The doctrine of reincarnation has an ethical value, though as nothing is inherited except the bare form of identity and our liabilities, it hardly amounts to a survival of personality. It does not fit in very well with other parts either of Hinduism or Buddhism, and is not now held with much conviction. The original Brahmanic teaching knew nothing of liberation from the cycle of rebirths, and Gautama is said to have refused to enter Nirvana while anyone remained unenlightened on earth. This last principle would carry us past Plato into Christianity—incarnational religion.

It would however be true that we nearly all regard the busy, hustling, acquisitive life of the west European and American as a huge mistake. We could say with the Old Testament prophet, "Wherefore do ye spend your money on that which is not bread, and your labour on that which satisfieth not?" We speak of the path of pursuit as a lower path than the path of renunciation or detachment, and we hold this not only on the familiar ground that the wise man has few wants, but because the path of pursuit implies alienation from and competition with others. It implies a wrong idea of personality.

During the Middle Ages in Europe the ethics of renunciation, an essential part of the original Gospel, prevailed over the ethics of world-affirmation. The motive of trying to bring about a better future for humanity was absent; the general opinion was that the end of the world was soon coming, and a good thing too. Since the Renaissance there has been a great reaction. A temper of secular optimism has thrown into the background the element of renunciation which was present in the teaching of Jesus, and which was acceptable to an age when civilisation was visibly breaking up. Especially in the countries which accepted the Reformation it came to be assumed that Jesus intended to found a Kingdom of God on this earth, to be brought about by human effort. By degrees the West became absorbed in the path of pursuit. The majority no longer had any interest in the philosophy of religion, no world-view; they thought only of man and human society, and almost identified goodness with what we call the lower path—morality touched with emotion and a respectable worldliness. The secular religion of the nineteenth century was a belief in what is called progress. Now the bottom has fallen out of this faith; Europe is disillusioned and perplexed. India has learned something from Europe; I venture to think that Europe has now much to learn from India.

Most Indian thinkers would probably accept the following declaration of faith. "I believe in one all-including, all-pervading, ever-complete, timeless, spaceless, universal soul or spirit or self, which is absolute and changeless, which is also identical with and includes within itself all the countless individual selves, and whose eternally changeless and yet ever-changing ideation the entire world-process of all souls and bodies is."* The following sentences from the Upanishads are often quoted: "The soul of created beings is a unity, only divided between creature and creature; unity and plurality at the same time, like the moon mirrored in many waters." "Who sees himself in all beings, and in himself all beings sees, enters into the highest Brahman without any other reason." "The highest Brahman, the soul of all, the great mainstay of the universe, more subtle than the subtle, the eternal Being, that art thou, that thou art" (*Tat twam asi*).†

This is what philosophers call an uncompromising Monism. All reality is one, and wisdom consists in complete detachment from all particular interests, which are barriers dividing us from reality. This is of course the path followed by exclusive mystics of all ages and countries. Every particular knowledge is discarded as inadequate and so a hindrance. *Neti, neti*—not this, they say, like the *nescio, nescio* of Bernard's famous hymn.

And what is the character which this view of life promotes? I will read you a few lines from Sir Edwin Arnold's translation of our famous classic, the "Bhaga-vadgita".

> "One who is freed
> In all his works from prickings of desire,
> Burned clean in act by the white fire of truth,
> The wise call that man wise; and such an one,
> Renouncing fruit of deeds, always content,

* Bhagavan Das, in *Contemporary Indian Philosophy*, p. 141.
† Schweitzer, *Indian Thought*, p. 35.

Always self-satisfying, if he works,
Doth nothing that shall stain his separate soul,
Which, quit of fear and hope, subduing self,
Rejecting outward impulse, yielding up
To body's need nothing save body, dwells
Sinless amid all sin, with equal calm
Taking what may befall, by grief unmoved,
Unmoved by joy, unenvyingly; the same
In good and evil fortunes, nowise bound
By bond of deeds."

Or this:—

"Humbleness, truthfulness and harmlessness,
Patience and honour, reverence for the wise,
Purity, constancy, control of self,
Contempt of sense-delights, self-sacrifice . . .
Detachment, lightly holding unto home,
Children and wife, and all that bindeth men;
An ever tranquil heart in fortunes good
And fortunes evil, with a will set firm
To worship Me, Me only, ceasing not;
Loving all solitudes, and shunning noise
Of foolish crowds; endeavours resolute
To reach perception of the Utmost Soul,
And grace to understand what gain it were
So to attain. This is true wisdom, Prince;
And what is otherwise is ignorance."*

Well, my Lord, you have asked my advice, and you
shall have it. We are old friends; I remember how
sincerely you wished to learn something of the wisdom
of the East when you governed a province in India. I

* Quoted by Urwick, *The Message of Plato*, pp. 69 and 88.

wish there were more like you. You English have given us what we never had before—justice, efficiency, and a splendid integrity. But most of your officials have never understood us or even wished to understand us. You have tried to give us what you believed in yourselves— good government, democracy, and freedom—the last by instalments. These are not words to conjure with in India, except for our chattering Babus. So now I am to be the Guru of an Indian governor. It is a great honour, but I do not shrink from it, for I think I see clearly.

You have had a normal human life, and have served your generation worthily. You have been a husband and father—that, for an Indian, is a duty not to be avoided. You have practised the political and practical virtues, and have filled a high position with distinction. Now the time has come for you to acquire the higher wisdom, which can be won only in retirement and detachment from all worldly interests. You probably know of Indians who, after filling important official posts, have decided to spend their old age in contemplation. Some of them have become ascetics, but that is not necessary. Believe me, circumstances have pointed the way to what is for your own highest good. You are not altogether a stranger to the mystical quest, but you have not yet gone far on the road. You are still a hale man for your age, and probably have several years before you. I beg you to spend them in contemplation of the eternal verities. I am not suggesting that you should adopt our religion. Mystics are all of the same faith, and you will find all you want in Christianity. But try to forget the desperate state of the world, which you can do nothing to remedy. From the highest point of view these things do not matter. "Man walketh in a vain shadow and disquieteth himself in vain," as one of your psalms says. This world is only a vain shadow, a drifting chaos. Find your rest where alone rest can be found, in the calm ocean of eternal Being.

WINTERBOURNE My dear Chandra, or as I should say my revered Guru, I am very much obliged to you. I believe your advice is good. But perhaps you hardly realise how difficult it is for an Englishman to live the life of contemplation. All our lives we have taught ourselves to think that to sit still with our hands before us is idleness. Of course it is not; thinking is hard work, and a form of activity. But it is very difficult for us, and though you Indians seem able to make a sudden change in your habits, from active business to contemplation, it would not come easy to me. Nor can I really agree with you that the ruin of our civilisation and the hideous crimes of the Germans against humanity do not matter. I know the mystics feel like that; "the actors only change their masks," as Plotinus says; but that is a degree of detachment which is beyond me, and what is more, I don't want to feel that I don't care. Such a man, as Euripides says, "suffers less, but we cannot envy his happiness".* Still, I believe you are right, and I must try to make a good use of the short time when I am laid on the shelf. Once more I thank you heartily, and I will try to do what you tell me.

PERRY Before my two fellow-guests arrived our host and I were discussing methods of escape from distressful circumstances. After a few frivolous remarks of mine about boredom, suggested by the behaviour

* Euripides, Andromache 420. ἧσσον μεν ἀλγεῖ, δυστυχῶν δ' εὐδαιμονεῖ.

of my travelling companions, I raised the question whether we can escape into the past by studying history. I suppose we may assume that in the mind of a superior Being past, present, and future are equally real. "All that is at all lasts ever past recall," as Browning says. "Nothing that *is* can ever perish," say the Platonists. We agreed that archaists who try to revive the past are generally a nuisance and that pinchbeck Napoleons are worse than a nuisance. That is partly because the past which they want to imitate is generally "une fable convenue", as Napoleon said of history. To carve the past at the joints, which is the business of the historian, is not easy. Having disposed of archaism, I suppose we ought to consider futurism, a subject which seems to belong to the Bishop as an exponent of Christianity. But first I should like to know what he thinks of the wisdom of the East as expounded by the Pundit.

WALDEGRAVE   I was of course much impressed by what he said. Mysticism is the heart of religion. But I think there is a danger in denying all value to our life in time. A journey through the unreal is an unreal journey. If the starting-point is empty, the goal will be empty too. Is there nothing between the deceiving phantasmagoria of the senses and the shoreless ocean of Nirvana? I should call this pannihilism. And does not the defect of this philosophy show itself by calm acquiescence in remediable social evils? The Indian sage is benevolent, but does his religion make him actively beneficent? He eats and drinks religiously, but does he not sometimes sin religiously? Of course I know that in practice the best Indians have beautiful characters, but I think their world-view is open to criticism.

CHANDRA Some of us are open to that criticism, but not all.

WALDEGRAVE I think the crucial question is whether we ought to detach ourselves from human love and affection. Many of the mystics have said Yes. They have been known to rejoice when death relieved them of family ties which, they thought, came between them and the love of God; they have been quite indifferent to disasters which threatened their country. Plotinus and Spinoza both express almost callous indifference to public misfortunes. In our day Einstein has confessed that he has "never belonged to my country, my home, my friends, or even to my family, with a whole heart". No doubt love often hurts. But is it the business of philosophy or religion to make us invulnerable? Christianity emphatically says not, and adds that human love is the chief hierophant of the divine mysteries. "He that loveth not his brother whom he hath seen, how shall he love God whom he hath not seen?"

PERRY Many thanks, Bishop. Now let us hear a discussion of futurism as an escape. Rather a mouthful for you, I am afraid.

WALDEGRAVE Yes, it is. It is now much more important than archaism, but it has not always been so. In classical antiquity, in spite of the popular cults of the spirits of the dead, it played only a small part, except in the Orphic brotherhoods, to which Platonism was affiliated. We gather from Plato's *Republic* that the average young Athenian in his day had not been taught to believe in the immortality of the soul. The earlier Hebrew religion had no doctrine of the last things. The shadowy Sheol was outside Jehovah's jurisdiction, and was as comfortless an abode as

Homer's Hades. The Jews certainly looked for an earthly future, in which their nation would bruise its neighbours with a rod of iron; this was not so much aggressive patriotism as a conviction that divine justice —reward and punishment—must somehow and somewhen be executed on earth. They acknowledged their own failings, and were prepared to believe that only a "remnant" would be saved. As the prospects of the nation grew darker, apocalyptism succeeded prophecy, and men's thoughts turned to a supernatural deliverance, a "day of the Lord". A common view was that the Messiah would come to reign on earth for a limited time, after which would occur the general resurrection and the "kingdom of God". Christianity succeeded to a mixed inheritance of Hellenistic thought, mainly Platonic and Stoic with an infusion of Oriental cults, and of the Judaism of the Dispersion, already influenced by Greek ideas. Its doctrines about the future were confused and inconsistent, mainly supramundane, though there were sporadic outbreaks of Millenarianism. The doctrine of the Church crystallised at one of the most dismal periods of history, at a time when as Julian the Apostate said the world was at its last gasp. This pessimism was an important psychological cause of the decline and fall of the Empire. It is quite as prominent in the pagans, in Julian, for example, as in the Christian writers.

Christian futurism was a way of escape, but not a very consolatory one, for it was commonly taught that only a minority would escape the torments of hell. It is difficult to say how far the lurid pictures of bliss and torment were believed in; but at any rate heaven and hell were treated as places, and the time of divine reward and punishment was in the future.

All eschatology is necessarily symbolical, though religious symbols, unlike those of poetry, are unconscious and intercalated in the time-process. But we now realise that heaven is not a place which we could reach in an aeroplane if we knew the way, and that eternity is not a series of moments snipped off at one end but not at the other. "Eye hath not seen nor ear heard." "It doth not yet appear what we shall be." In the first century dogma had not petrified.

In the early modern period, as soon as secular optimism flourished, the belief in a supramundane future began to decay. In the eighteenth century the belief in human perfectibility, the last great Western heresy as it has been called, made heaven and hell seem superfluous and unreal. This was a superstition, but it undoubtedly encouraged human effort. "The century of hope" was a time of wonderful achievement. But public affairs have killed the superstition, and as there has been no revival of belief in a future life we seem to be threatened with another period when men will "have no hope", and be "without God in the world". Secularism, says the French historian Ozanam, "promises an earthly paradise at the end of a flowery path, and gives us a premature hell at the end of a way of blood".

Millenarianism, which, as I have said, broke out sporadically at various times in Church history, chiefly among the sects rather than in the great Church, has appeared in a modern form as the writing of Utopias. The older Utopias were usually placed in some distant country; the newer in some not very distant time. Socialism and Communism are utopian visions of the near future. Most of them are pictures of a terminal state, not of a progressive society; this stamps them as.

27

dreams which can have no fulfilment; they are secularised apocalypses.

The extravagant prophecies of unending progress towards perfection, common in nineteenth-century literature, and not least in the writings of men of science like Herbert Spencer, have been often collected for our amusement and surprise. Now that the superstition is practically dead, we can consider calmly whether secular futurism can reasonably give us any comfort.

Ultimately, of course, all life on this earth must cease. The dead moon is there to warn us of our own inevitable fate. It is odd that the Second Law of Thermodynamics, which the French call the principle of Carnot, was as well known to the nineteenth-century optimists as it is to us; but they did not like to think of it. The universe, science tells us, is running down like a clock. If anyone doubts this, says Eddington, he puts himself out of court. I am not a man of science, but it does occur to me that if a clock is running down it must have been wound up by somebody, and that whatever unknown agency wound it up once may presumably wind it up again. Otherwise it seems to me that this theory demands that the universe started with a bang at some date which we could give if we knew it; and though this might satisfy a traditionalist Christian, it is a rather unwelcome admission for a scientist. However, I will leave this problem, since I am not competent to deal with it.

Although the doom of our earth is certain, we have probably an enormously long lease. Our species is still in the stage of the rattle and feeding-bottle. It is possible, no doubt, that our sun may blow up and become a *nova*, as happens to a few stars, I believe, every year. Or a roving star may barge into our sun, as, according to Jeans, happened once when the planets were born. But both are said to be very unlikely. We may then reasonably expect that our race will have abundant time to try every possible and impossible experiment in politics and economics. It is very probable that there will be more flowering times of civilisation worthy to be compared with the ages of Pericles, Augustus, Louis XIV, and I should add with that of Victoria. There will also be glacial epochs, both spiritual and physical. Some of the arts have perhaps reached perfection; but there will, we may reasonably hope, be progress, real progress, local, sporadic, and short-lived, again and again in the long future. And some of its achievements may, we hope, be permanent possessions.

There are, however, two other possibilities. Let us fancy a future historian on the planet Venus, which we will suppose to have become cool enough to support intelligent life, writing in the following strain : "On the planet between ourselves and Mars a very remarkable, perhaps unique episode occurred, in the almost complete domination of the planet, for a short period of about fifteen thousand years, by one of the larger apes. This species, by the possession of superior cunning, gained an ascendancy over all the other living creatures on the planet. It used this power to deface in a revolting manner the beauties of this picturesque globe, and to exterminate many other species which except in craft and cruelty were superior to itself. There were signs that under State Socialism these apes might advance or degenerate into automata; they had apparently set before themselves as an ideal the polity of the social insects. But this change, which would have pegged them down for ages in the same degenerate condition, was anticipated by their success in exploiting their knowledge of chemistry to produce substances which could annihilate their centres of population wholesale. By making the fullest use of these discoveries they procured their own extinction. Our theologians are fond of pointing to the extermination of this noxious species as a convincing proof of the operation of divine providence in history."

PERRY Well, Bishop, I am glad none of your episcopal brethren are here to listen to you. I am not sure that as a government official Lord Winterbourne ought not to report you to your Metropolitan. We are all shocked.

WALDEGRAVE Well, well, we are all in mufti now. The other possibility is, of course, that we may reach a state of stable equilibrium, like the bees, ants, and termites. Then we should not say *"Cogito, ergo sum,"* but *"Non cogito, ergo sum"*. Thought will be a fatal handicap when instinct supplies all our needs. A suffragette millennium, a gynæcocracy of maiden aunts— how would that be for the heirs of all the ages? What is to prevent it? Only our incorrigible habit of trying to live beyond our incomes. But seriously, the new reign of the machine may put a stop to human progress. Man the tool-maker has not been a great biological success. The Cro-Magnon skulls have a greater brain capacity than that of the modern *homo sapiens*. There are many things which the handy man could formerly do for himself, and which the despised savage can still do for himself, but which the modern man would be quite helpless if he were confronted with. "You press the button, we do the rest." We may end by losing all our faculties except the knowledge of which button to press. At last, if we are Americans, comes the "mortician", with "you kick the bucket, we do the rest".

WINTERBOURNE You know, Bishop, that I asked you to come because I am not very happy, and need your help. Escape into the future, for me, does not mean the hope, or dream, of a better world after the war. I fear that such hopes are likely to be bitterly disappointed. What it means for me is "the blessed hope of everlasting life", and I think you may be able to help me to think more clearly about this. What we were told as children was intelligible enough, but difficult to believe.

WALDEGRAVE I know, my dear Lord Winter-bourne, and I ought not to have amused myself by laughing at the perfectionists. But the subject is terribly difficult. In the last resort, it depends on the most perplexing and controversial of all philosophical problems, the relation of time to eternity. At the present time, when for too easily intelligible reasons there has been a lamentable revival of necromancy, in company with astrology and other superstitions, one has to be careful not to wound the lacerated hearts of the bereaved. But I am not afraid of this in your case. The kind of survival which Sir Oliver Lodge and his disciples comforted themselves with imagining would add a new terror to death. It is the dream of an aching heart; none would desire it for himself.

Until we understand the meaning of "God is Spirit", we are not free from an insidious residue of materialism—the notion that spirit is the most rarefied form of matter, and therefore amenable to "scientific evidence". The moment we are asked to accept scientific evidence for spiritual truth, the alleged spiritual truth becomes neither spiritual nor true. It is degraded into an event in the phenomenal world, and when so degraded it cannot be substantiated.

Christian teaching has always been confused on this subject. The Church tried to combine the late Jewish belief in a resurrection of the body with the Greek belief in the immortality of the soul. It thus found room for two modes of faith, but never quite reconciled them. Jewish religion always linked itself with time and history; Greek thought rested on an ideal-real invisible and unchanging world. Reality for the Greek was timeless; for the Jew it was a temporal order controlled by catastrophic divine interventions. I am not enough of a philosopher to discuss the aspects of truth which each of these world-views embodies, and I don't think you want a metaphysical lecture. But this much I want to say.

The belief in God is central; the belief in immortality is peripheral. All arguments for a future life which are independent of belief in God are illusory. Some of the reasons which are given are not good enough to be true. If I desire a future life because I enjoy my existence here and wish to prolong it indefinitely, that has nothing to do with religion. If I desire a future life because I am miserable and think I have a claim to compensation, that is not religion either. If I have made certain investments in good works on which I hope to make a handsome profit—"whatever, Lord, we lend to thee repaid a thousandfold will be"—that has no more to do with religion than if I invested my money on the faith of one of the similarly worded prospectuses which I used to find on my breakfast-table. A very common argument is that our lives here are incomplete, and that we must have an opportunity of perfecting our characters. The idea of progress in eternity is rather new in Christianity. It belongs to the perfectibility theory of which I have spoken. Like purgatory, it may be true, but we do not know. Robert Browning, the Pundit will remember, believed in re-incarnation.

> "And I shall thereupon
> Take rest ere I begone
> Once more on my adventure brave and new."

In what way does belief in immortality depend on belief in God? It is because God has revealed himself as what Nicholas of Cusa calls the "Value of Values". The three absolute values, Goodness, Truth, and Beauty, are the revelation of his nature, and it is in them that we find our immortality. They are absolute because they stand in their own right, and cannot be made means to anything else, or even to each other, though together they are "a threefold cord not quickly broken". We have at least as good a right to believe in the objective reality of these values as to believe in the world as known to science. Indeed, we have a much better right; for the physical world is an abstraction useful for many purposes, but manifestly incomplete, because it deals only with the quantitative aspects of things, and disregards the imponderables which have a higher degree of reality.

Now these values are eternal and indestructible. They are super-temporal, and so far as we can identify ourselves with them we are sure of our immortality. If we were wholly inside time we should not know anything about time; we are not conscious of the movement of the earth through space because we and

33   C

our environment are carried round together. We can live, "in heart and mind," in the eternal spiritual world because it is our true home, though not our present place of residence. We are "strangers and pilgrims" here, but "our citizenship is in heaven".

WINTERBOURNE   That, Bishop, is in agreement with St. John's language about eternal life as a present possession. "We have passed from death unto life because we love the brethren." "This is life eternal, that they should know thee, the only true God." But futurism seems here to be excluded, and perhaps activity also, if we have only to apprehend eternally existing values. The Indians have discovered the Fourth Gospel, and it delights them.

WALDEGRAVE   It is quite true that two of the absolute values, Truth and Beauty, seem to be essentially timeless; but the third, Goodness, speaks to us in the imperative mood. Morality is a matter of will, and time is the form of the will. In heaven, I suppose, there is no morality, for morality lives in the conflict with evil; but here we are fellow-workers with God in the cosmic duel. Things happen in time; things have to be done; as moral beings time, and progress too, have a meaning for us. And yet, in so far as we obey the true, practise the good, and love the beautiful, we are citizens of heaven, where there is no more death, neither sorrow nor crying.

WINTERBOURNE   How about future reward and punishment?

WALDEGRAVE   I do not think these should occupy our minds much. The crudity of popular pictures of heaven and hell has done much harm; the Father of our Lord Jesus Christ cannot reward and punish in this way. The appropriate reward of a life of dis-

34

interested service and love is not residence in a city with streets of gold, and the appropriate punishment of selfishness and vice is not to be roasted in an oven. We shall reap what we have sown. "Sow an action and reap a habit; sow a habit and reap a character; sow a character and reap a destiny."

WINTERBOURNE Ought we then to try to get rid of the idea of a *future* life altogether?

WALDEGRAVE I think not, though we must not identify eternal life with survival. Many people have welcomed the thought of eternity as changeless, in contrast with the changes and chances of mortal life. But nothing is gained by getting rid of the idea of flux, merely to substitute for it the idea of immobility. It might even look like preferring death to life. The subject is very difficult, but as perpetuity is the time-form of eternity, and time (as Plato says) its moving image, and as we are now on our probation in a world of time, I frankly allow myself to think of heaven as a future state, and I do not forbid myself the hope that we may there be reunited to the loved ones who have gone before us. We ought to banish materialistic symbols from our religion as much as possible; materialistic dogmatism is only the clerical form of dogmatic materialism; but we need not impoverish our religion by jealously forbidding faith to speak in its own language, which is charged with poetry and myth.

WINTERBOURNE The New Testament is much more agnostic than popular theology. "Now we see through a glass darkly." "Now are we the sons of God, and it doth not yet appear what we shall be." "Eye hath not seen, nor ear heard, neither hath it entered into the heart of man to conceive, what God hath prepared

35

for them that love him." I believe it is better for us not to know too much, though I wish we did not know so little.

PERRY There is one question that I should like to ask. Keyserling says that mysticism always ends in an impersonal immortality. Is this true? I think it is true of Indian mysticism, which tends to wipe out all boundary lines.

WINTERBOURNE I also should like to hear the answer to that question. Though my life is ending rather sadly, I don't quite want to resign "this pleasing anxious being" for good and all.

WALDEGRAVE Well, what is personality? Leibnitz gave us a world of spiritual atoms, without windows, like the hard impenetrable little billiard balls of a discarded physics. That is certainly not the view of the Indians, nor, I should say, of Christian philosophy. The conception of an abstract ego seems to me to involve three assumptions, none of which is true. The first is that there is a sharp line separating subject from object, and from other subjects. The second is that the subject, sundered from the object, remains unchanged through time. The third is that this indiscerptible entity is in some mysterious way both myself and my property. I should maintain that the centres of consciousness flow freely into each other even here, while in the spiritual world there are probably no barriers at all. The empirical self is by no means identical throughout, and that part of us which St. Paul calls Spirit and the Platonists Nous is only ours potentially; it is what we may become when we rise above mere psychic existence. As to whether it is "my" soul that hopes to go to heaven, I can give no meaning to the question at all. The mystics would

36

like to expunge "I" and "mine" from their vocabulary;
and our Lord tells us that we must lose our "soul"
(*psyche*) in order to save it. Impersonality is a negative
conception; what it negates, or should negate, is the
imprisonment of the soul in a cell without windows.
The more "organic filaments" we can throw out, the
more personal we become.

Nevertheless, I think the majority of the Indians go
too far. In religion, the relation between man and
God is always an "I" and "thou" relationship.

CHANDRA   We think that at last we discover that
"I" and "thou" are one.

WALDEGRAVE   And then what room is there for
the love of God? It becomes a kind of Narcissism. And
what room is there for love of our brethren? Sympathy,
yes; but there must be two to love each other. From
our point of view, you Indians buy your invulnerability
too dear. May we not suppose that in heaven there is
distinctness without separation, complete harmony
without confusion? I am very fond of a famous passage
in Plotinus. In heaven "everyone has all things in himself and sees all things in another, so that all things
are everywhere and all is all and each is each, and
infinite the glory". But he insists that individuality is
not extinguished in the world "yonder".

WINTERBOURNE   There is one more question that
I should like to ask you, Chandra. The later Platonists
were exercised as to whether it would have been better
for the soul to remain in the spiritual world. The best
answer, perhaps, was that of Proclus: the soul came
down, "wishing to imitate the providence of the gods".
You have let fall a hint that Buddha could not be
content to go to heaven alone. The Bishop will remember how this was the one thing that St. Augustine

37

could not find in his reading of the Platonists. Well, would it be a tenable view that the mystic quest is all right, but that it is only half the story? Just as the three apostles on the Mount of Transfiguration were not allowed to stay there, but were bidden to go down into the plain, where there was a demon waiting for them to cast out, so the contemplative must consider that his vision was meant to inspire a task, and is incomplete until it has borne fruit in action for others. This alternation of contemplation and action, answering to each other, may be part of the everlasting systole and diastole of the universe—a fanciful idea of my own. What would your philosophers say to that?

CHANDRA Some of them would approve; but frankly, we are escapists, and the attractions of a dreamless slumber in the bosom of the Eternal are too strong for us. I think I am prepared to admit that Christianity, with its doctrine of the Incarnation, has put the keystone in the arch. But I am not tempted to join any of your Churches.

PERRY I should have liked to hear more about Plato's escape "to our dear country", which is rather different from that of the Indians, though they had much in common, and different also from Christian teaching. The essence of Platonism, if I understand it, is that subject and object must be transformed together. If we see things as they are we shall live as we ought, and if we live as we ought we shall see things as they are. The faculty which sees things as they are is one which "all possess but few use"; it is the whole personality acting under the guidance of its highest part. The fully real can be fully known, and those who are filled with the most real are most really filled. The beginning and end of the journey are simple; the intermediate stage is complex. Clement of Alexandria, the Christian Platonist, calls the three stages Faith, Knowledge, and Love. In order to reach the highest stage, the soul in love must become spirit; the discipline is long and hard. I think the main difference from Indian thought is that the Platonist rises *through* the things of time, the moving image of eternity, instead of turning away from them; and that in consequence his "intelligible world" is full of colour and movement, unlike Nirvana. I like the Quaker Pennington's words: "Every truth is a shadow except the last. But every truth is substance in its own place, though it be but a shadow in another place. And the shadow is a true shadow, as the substance is a true substance".

WINTERBOURNE   Well done, Perry, I did not know you studied the old philosophers. What do you say, Bishop? Is not this sacramental view of the world very satisfying?

WALDEGRAVE   I think it would be in normal times. But now "the whole world lieth in the wicked one", and we are tempted to look for a more drastic way of escape. Still, I believe he is right. We want more courage; I know I do. Things looked pretty black for St. Paul when he wrote those splendidly defiant words in the eighth chapter of Romans, and for St. Augustine when he wrote his "City of God". I like his summing up of the success of the Romans: "*Acceperunt mercedem suam, vani vanam*". They had their reward, and it turned to dust and ashes. They took the sword and perished by the sword, as I believe the Germans will some day, but we shall hardly live to see it.

WINTERBOURNE   My three friends, you have all done me good. I shall not take the bowl of the Indian

39

ascetic, but I shall live very simply and quietly, and give more time to prayer and meditation. I think I understand how the Bishop would have me prepare for death and for what comes afterwards. We know hardly anything ; our Lord's parables are not descriptions of actual facts; but we know a good deal of the nature of God as He has revealed it to men, and we have the promise of the Holy Spirit to help us. I shall not get far in the contemplative life; I have lived too much in and for the world; but I think I can bear a few years of inaction and loneliness, especially if you will deign to visit me in the humble cottage which I must try to find somewhere.

MIRACLE, MYTH
AND MYSTERY

SCENE: *Price's rooms at St. Thomas's College, Oxford.*

SPEAKERS: *Price, 35, Fellow and Tutor of St. Thomas's;
Edwards, 35, a London journalist; Smyth, 47, formerly
Dean of St. Thomas's, now an honorary canon and rector
of Slimeham in the Sludge, Norfolk, a College living;
Johnson, 21, a senior scholar of St. Thomas's.*

TIME: *Before the War.*

PRICE   Edwards, do you remember the talks we
used to have in your rooms, when you meant to
become a clergyman?

EDWARDS   I do indeed.

PRICE   Do you ever regret having changed your
mind?

EDWARDS   I do every day of my life. But I had no
choice. No bishop would have looked at me.

SMYTH   Why? What were your difficulties? You
never brought them to me.

EDWARDS   I did not dare, Padre, though you were
not a dignitary of the Church then. You would have
been horrified.

SMYTH   My dear man, I am not so easily shocked.
Tell us; I am interested.

EDWARDS   Well, if you will have it. I thought then,
and I am sure now, that the most sublime spiritual
revelation ever made to mankind has been travestied,

vulgarised, made incredible by its custodians. The immortality of the soul has turned into been ἡ ἀνάστασις τῶν νεκρῶν, the standing up of the corpses. The divine beauty of our Lord's character has been interpreted on the analogy of the least edifying pagan myths. His triumph over death has been explained to mean that his dead body walked out of its grave, after putting on the clothes which the angels brought with them—this, if I remember right, is the answer of St. Thomas Aquinas to a perfectly reasonable question; and that after a few days he flew away to an Olympus beyond the moon. These fairy-tales, which as far as I can see have no more to do with religion than Jack and the Beanstalk, must be accepted *ex animo* as physical facts by all who wish to be ministers of Christ.

SMYTH There would certainly be a rumpus at Slimeham in the Sludge if you were their rector. You say that these dogmas have nothing to do with religion?

EDWARDS I do say so. Take the virgin birth, which by the way is only half insisted on by Anglicans. The Catholic doctrine is that after the birth of Jesus the hymen of his mother was found to be intact. "Forth he came, as light through glass", as an old carol says. The bishops do not ask candidates whether they believe that. Now suppose that a case of parthenogenesis in man were fully authenticated. There would be a tremendous commotion in medical and scientific circles, and I fear there would be a large crop of "miraculous" births. But would such a phenomenon prove anything of interest to religion?

SMYTH I am not sure that I agree with you that it has nothing to do with religion. The theory is that as our Lord was unique it is reasonable to believe the evidence that his birth was miraculous. Our theologians do not suggest that he was a hybrid between a deity and a mortal woman. That would be paganism, and of course the offspring of such a union would be a demigod, not "perfect God and perfect man". I assure you that many educated people find no difficulty in accepting the tradition.

EDWARDS Whom do you mean by educated people? Old ladies in the precincts? Retired Colonels?

SMYTH It happens that my squire at Slimeham is a retired Colonel or rather a General, a very distinguished soldier. His beliefs are just those which you consider absurd; he is strong on the empty tomb. He is not only a devout Christian, but one of the most level-headed men that I know.

EDWARDS If he is what you say, could you not explain to him that these miracles are terrible stumbling-blocks to many people, and that the religion of Christ can stand more firmly without them?

SMYTH No, indeed I could not. The squire would say that if I cannot believe the fundamental doctrines of the Church it is my duty as an honest man to resign my commission. And that would be the end of our friendship.

EDWARDS But you do not think that his faith is really based on these alleged portents in the natural order. How could it be?

SMYTH I suppose not, but he says so.

JOHNSON Would you say that he is rationalising convictions which really rest on what Quakers call the inner light?

PRICE I think not. This may be the way the doctrines started. The Church honoured its Founder with every tribute that the faith and love of that age could

43

suggest. But in our age of science no one would think that an Incarnation would necessarily be attended by signs of this kind.

EDWARDS Then how do you explain the survival of these beliefs?

PRICE Most of us want a bridge tó take us across from the seen to the unseen, from the world of facts to the world of values, from the temporal to the eternal, from appearance to reality—put it how you will. A few mystics are content to live on the other side; a much larger number of worldlings "mind earthly things" and do not wish to cross. But most of us do want a bridge. Must we make our own? No, there is an old bridge, which has carried the traffic for centuries.

EDWARDS But can they help asking whether it still bears?

SMYTH That is exactly what they are afraid to do. They do not trust themselves to decide. A busy man, as Carlyle says, cannot waste time in verifying his ready reckoner. Besides, must faith be rational?

PRICE Ah, there we come to the big philosophical problem which perhaps underlies the whole discussion. What do you say, Johnson? Must religion be rational?

JOHNSON Your Greats pupils have of course often discussed that. I think none of us believe in the materialism of the last century. You have taught us that the affirmations of religious experience are among the factors of which philosophy has to take account. We remember Bradley's impressive words on this point. Dogmatic naturalism seems to be breaking up from within. We have read writers like John Haldane, who wish to revive what they don't like to call vitalism.

44

They believe in epigenesis—Kant's word, isn't it?—
rather than in evolution. I mean that a new factor
must come in with life and consciousness. And is not a
new factor a kind of miracle?

PRICE   Do you read the astronomers too?

JOHNSON   Yes, Eddington and Jeans; and I must
say they have shaken my faith in the philosophy of
science. They begin, it seems to me, with naive
common-sense realism—stars and atoms as concrete
realities—and end with an outmoded Berkleyan idealism. Is there not a hiatus somewhere in their argument,
Mr. Price?

PRICE   I think there is. Miss Stebbing has trounced
them severely.

JOHNSON   I have not read her book, but I was much
amused by Harvey Wickham's *Unrealists*. He guys all
the most revered prophets of modern thought. The
latest physics, he says, has abolished the dog and the
tail, leaving only the wag.

PRICE   Yes, or the grin without the Cheshire cat.
But we must not suppose that materialism is disproved
because matter has been "defecated to a transparency".

JOHNSON   I understand that. But must we accept
the irrational? Meyerson says that we must just accept
several brute facts which cannot be rationalised. But
I know you quarrel with the Germans for glorifying
the irrational.

PRICE   So I do. There is nothing irrational in
admitting that there are some things which we
cannot account for.

JOHNSON   I am glad you say that. One or two of
us read Karl Barth.

PRICE   Well, don't. That is the road to Dayton,
Tennessee.

45

SMYTH But, Price, about those facts which we have to accept without trying to explain them. What are they?

PRICE Well, there is the existence of the world. Why is there a world, and how did it come into existence, if it ever did? And Time and Place. Einstein and Alexander have married them; I sometimes think that marriage may end in a divorce. At any rate Einstein protests that it is a physical or mathematical theory, not a philosophical explanation. And there are our dear old friends the ultimate, intrinsic or absolute values. Perhaps we may say there is God himself.

SMYTH But these are the most important of all facts. If we must just accept them as they are, how shall we relate them to the world of change and move-ment, of cause and effect?

PRICE That, I think, is where Plato comes in with his myths. It is one of his great merits that he dis-cerned that we cannot do without myths, even in philosophy.

SMYTH Then, without prejudice to the question whether the miracles of the Creed are factually true or not—and modern science is chary of using the word "impossible"—their value to us is as symbols of eternal and timeless truth. They are an indispensable "bridge", as Price told us so well. And I suppose we may say that a true bridge is one that will take us across, just as a true pair of spectacles is a pair that enables us to read. The old saying "true for you" seems to have a meaning.

JOHNSON Padre, that is William James at his worst. Is our tutor going to allow rank pragmatism to be preached to his pupils?

PRICE   I do not think pragmatism is the right conclusion. I like St. Paul's admission that now we see by symbols (enigmas) as in a mirror. It is only when we are in contact with ultimate realities that we need symbolism. There is plenty of it in art and poetry; but beauty is one of the ultimates.

EDWARDS   I am not satisfied. I am not satisfied at all. There is nothing symbolic or mythical about these dogmas. You and I perhaps may find a deep symbolic meaning in them; I agree that it may be found quite easily. But those who believe in them repudiate such an interpretation indignantly. They insist that the miracles are objective facts in the visible world, and that if they were not they would care nothing for them. That Christ was born without a human father is a fact of the same kind as that other infants are born in the normal manner. Ask any traditionalist, or any rationalist, whether you are not wriggling out of the difficulty.

SMYTH   Will you answer, Price? I confess that I am rather perplexed.

PRICE   As articles of religious faith they are clearly not in the same class as other events. If they were, people would not feel so strongly about them. Rationalists of course wish to pin us down to the question of physical fact; they want to discredit Christianity. The orthodox agree with them, because they do not want to see their bridge meddled with; they call the miracles the foundations of their faith. In dogmatic architecture the foundations are ingeniously supported by the superstructure. In other words, they are not really the foundations at all.

JOHNSON   But is there not another explanation? I forget who it was who said that supernaturalism is the mysticism of the materialist. Is there not some truth in that?

PRICE I am afraid there is.

SMYTH Those who consolidated the dogmas of the Church were certainly not materialists. May we not say that miracle, which a German philosopher called "faith's dearest child", is the natural language of faith in a pre-scientific age, and is still the natural language of faith to a vast number of good people whom the Church has no right to offend or alienate?*

EDWARDS I doubt whether there are so many as you think, though I understand why many cling to tradition instead of thinking out a creed for themselves. But at any rate we are no longer at the stage when faith automatically creates myths. They are a terrible handicap. Let us have the courage and honesty to discard them. We do not need symbols any more.

PRICE You don't need symbols, Edwards? What is your picture of reality? Is it local, Here and Yonder ($\grave{\epsilon}\nu\tau\alpha\hat{\upsilon}\theta\alpha$ and $\grave{\epsilon}\kappa\hat{\epsilon}\hat{\iota}$), as Greek thought pictured it? Or is it temporal, Here and Hereafter? Or optical, Appearance and Reality? Or a mixture of all three, like Christian eschatology? Or, as some Indian philosophers are accused of doing, do you think of Appearance as an appearance of nothing, and Reality as the reality of nothing? Where do you expect to go to? To Valhalla, or the Elysian Fields, or the Intelligible World of the Platonists, or Paradise, or Nirvana?

EDWARDS Oh hang it, Socrates, I can't answer all those questions. I am a very poor philosopher, as you know. Only a second in Greats. If you have finished

* "Faith is a spring of unconscious poetry. When symbols become transparent they no longer bind." *Amiel.*

your hemlock—whisky I should say—I shall go to bed. But seriously, if the clergy would think a little more of the many good people who do not go to church, and why they stop away, I think they would do better. Churches die of arterio-sclerosis, and the symptoms seem to me very apparent. Good-night, all of you.

JOHNSON Padre, half of me thinks that Edwards is right, the other half that he is wrong. What ought I to think?

SMYTH Well, Johnson, you remember that St. Paul thinks of "the whole process of Christ", his life, death, resurrection and ascension, as a kind of drama which must be re-enacted in little in the experience of individual Christians. This has always been near to the heart of Christianity. It is the message of the German mystic, Angelus Silesius, who expounds it in metrical epigrams. It has lately been emphasised by the Russian theologian Berdyaeff. As for religious symbols—"factlike stories" as von Hügel calls them—though the problem is nearly always treated as one of natural science and the laws of nature, it is really metaphysical. What is the relation of the sensible world, which is a construction made by ourselves for our own needs out of very imperfect materials, to ultimate reality? I am afraid we must take refuge in the theologian's "asylum of ignorance", and call it a mystery. But I am poaching on your preserves, Price; I have forgotten what little philosophy I ever knew.

PRICE I don't think you have. I have never thought of it exactly in that way, but I believe you are right. Churches after all are secular institutions, in which the half-educated cater for the half-converted. (No reflection on you, Smyth!) They cannot be anything else.

There are not nearly enough philosophers and mystics to make a Church; and besides, philosophers and mystics do not need institutions, except for the sake of fellowship; they can stand on their own feet; they do not depend on authority. I don't envy the bishops, who have to enforce a standardised orthodoxy which the more intelligent among them must know to be a pitiful jumble of petrified symbols; but most of them soon learn their trade, and they have not much time to think. It is not as if philosophy had anything much better to give. Do you find much difficulty in preaching honest sermons, Smyth?

SMYTH Not a great deal; but perhaps I am one of your half-educated. If I am doing any good at Slimeham, I think it is mainly by the example of a pure and happy Christian home, for which I have to thank my wife, and by occasional private heart-to-heart talks. You have no idea how simple and yet how wise some of these rustics are. They often make me feel very humble.

AN URGENT TASK

A DISCUSSION SOCIETY: *The debate is opened by Woolman, a Quaker, who moves "That the total abolition of war is the most urgent and immediate task of civilisation".*

WOOLMAN   The debate which I have been asked to open may be and I hope will be conducted from different points of view. I can only speak as a Quaker, that is, as a Christian who regards the teaching of Christ as authoritative, but does not pay much respect to the authority of the great political Churches. There have been endless discussions as to whether Jesus forbade war absolutely. The answer seems to me clear, and I will make it as short as possible. His own words leave no room for doubt. "Blessed are the peacemakers." "Love your enemies." "Resist not the aggressor." "They that take the sword shall perish by the sword." These and other sayings seem quite decisive. Are there any qualifications?

I think only these. Our Lord certainly used the method of hyperbole. He told his disciples to turn the other cheek to the smiter. But when he was smitten himself he did not do so, but administered a gentle rebuke. (St. Paul, we remember, on a similar occasion was provoked to commit a refreshingly human contempt of court!)

He never said in so many words, "War is always sinful". It was not his way to give particular commands; he was content with general principles. Some think that he meant to be explicit about marriage and

51

divorce, and churchmen have been disputing ever since as to what he meant!

He said nothing about future ages; or if he did, which is not likely, his hearers, who were dreaming about "the age of the Messiah", would not have been interested and would soon have forgotten. But the notion that the morality of the Gospels was only an "Interimsethik" may, I am sure, be rejected.

St. Paul not only accepts the law of love as the method by which the Christian must try to overcome evil, but he sees clearly that internationalism follows from it. In Christ there is neither Jew nor Greek, barbarian, Scythian, bond nor free. It is quite a mistake to suppose that "love your enemies" applies only to private quarrels. The classical word for a public enemy is foreign to biblical Greek.

There is no deviation from this teaching in any book of the New Testament except the Apocalypse, which according to some scholars is in part a Jewish treatise. But, of course, the attitude of the Old Testament is quite different, though there are some noble predictions of a reign of peace in the prophets. It is to be hoped that no Christians any longer put the Old Testament on the same level as the New. But the literature of this half-civilised tribe is still appealed to far too often by the advocates of violence. A clergyman is quoted as saying, "The Sermon on the Mount was for the new kingdom, but since the world has rejected that kingdom, God has been obliged to go back to Old Testament methods". This saying deserves to be bracketed with the words of a Scottish minister: "The Almighty is obliged to do many things in his official capacity which he would scorn to do as a private individual".

The teaching of the Fathers of the Church about war has been so often collected that I will not trouble you with quotations. Put shortly, it would be true to say that before Constantine the condemnation of war and violence was almost unanimous, but that there were certainly a good many Christians in the army. The lost treatise of Celsus against the Christians, written toward the close of the second century, entreats the Christians not to be indifferent to the dangers which were already threatening the empire. The empire did not encourage the Christians to be very patriotic! They were human after all, and could not be pleased to see their friends thrown to the lions. But all through the age of the persecutions the Christian Church offered no resistance to the cruelty of the mob and of the officials, and gradually wore down the ill-will of the populace, till the last persecution, under Diocletian, failed largely because pagan public opinion revolted against it. It is the classical example of overcoming violence and injustice by gentleness.

The tone of the Church changed rapidly after Christianity became the religion of the State. I do not mean that the Church justified aggressive wars, but the rights of the State when attacked were recognised, and this was an age of barbarian invasions. Augustine uses an argument often employed since, that in stopping the aggressor we are acting in his true interest. But it is unfortunately true that a faithful acceptance of Christ's teaching has been found chiefly among small sects, not in the great Churches. Anabaptists, Albigenses, Mennonites, Quakers, Doukhobors—it is in such small and sometimes persecuted bodies that we find uncompromising pacifism. Honesty compels me to own that our founder, George Fox, was lukewarm about peace till the monarchy was restored. He wrote an amazing letter to Oliver Cromwell urging him to pursue his career of conquest. Andrew Marvell hardly went further.

There are a few examples in later history of the happy results of Christian methods. The best known is the action of the Quakers in North America during the Indian wars. The savages spared the Quakers as soon as they learnt that they were their friends. After the Great War the activities of the Friends on the Continent made a deep impression on our former enemies, and did something to counteract the disgust which the fierce invectives of our ecclesiastics had aroused against the religion which they professed. Quaker charities are usually well organised; their work in Poland was a thing to be proud of. We may also remember the rare acts of generosity on the part of nations, such as the gift of the Ionian Islands to Greece. These have not been thrown away.

Of course pacifists are accustomed to being heckled. We are asked, If you found a ruffian attacking your wife or daughter, would you resist? Of course we should, with a poker or any other handy weapon. If your house was being burgled, would you summon the police? Certainly I should. Are you in favour of unilateral disarmament, the consequence of which might be that we should lose our independence and be subject to the brutalities of a German army of occupation? That is a more difficult question, but I think I should answer as follows. If we were all saints, that would be the right course. We might for a time be a martyr nation, and we should no doubt be robbed. But I think the aggressors would soon be ashamed of themselves, and would leave us alone. But the typical

Englishman is not at all like St. Francis of Assisi, and if we disbanded our armed forces our rivals would say, "You are like a gambler who after winning a large stake proposes to play for love for the rest of the evening. That is a little too simple for us." But if after the Great War the Allies had treated the Germans as generously as Wellington and Castlereagh treated the French after Waterloo, I am convinced that there would have been no Hitler and no second World War. And if you ask me whether I should like my country-men to be all meek and mild, "as harmless as doves," well, there is a great deal of human nature even in a Quaker, and I think we must admit that although the absolute "Law of Nature", which is also the law of Christ, forbids war and violence, mankind "in a state of sin" cannot quite live up to it. This looks like giving away my case, and perfect consistency is really very difficult. But I believe that "overcome evil with good" is true Christianity.

But my thesis is that civilised nations ought to agree to put an end to war, and to do it at once. The alternative is utter ruin and a return of the Dark Ages. The large majority in every country would vote for it enthusiastically. Drucker, who knows the Continent, even says that the Germans dreaded war more than the democracies. I do not think this was true in 1914, but I think it may have been true in 1939. There was very little flag-wagging in any country at the outbreak of this war.

Can anyone doubt that war is the greatest of all human evils? Aldous Huxley says: "Every road to-wards a better state of society is blocked, sooner or later, by war, by threats of war, by preparations for war. That is the truth, the odious and inescapable truth."¹ Huxley adds that it is "obviously nonsensical" to say, with a well-known man of science, that war is nature's pruning-hook. War destroys the young and healthy and spares the weaklings. War is the most dysgenic of all agencies; "immer der Krieg verschlingt die Besten," as Schiller says. "Castile makes men and wastes them," says a Spanish writer. As for the destruction of wealth, I have copied out the words of a very wise American, Dr. Nicholas Murray Butler. With the money wasted in the Great War "we could have built a £500 house with £200 of furniture and placed it on five acres of land worth £20 an acre for every family in the United States, Canada, Australia, England, Wales, Ireland, Scotland, France, Belgium, Germany and Russia. There would have been enough left over to give every city of 20,000 inhabitants in all these countries a million-pound library and a two-million-pound university. Out of the balance we could have set aside a sum at five per cent interest which would have paid for all time a £200 salary for 125,000 teachers and 125,000 nurses. Having done all this we could still have bought up all France and Belgium and everything they possessed. That was the price paid twenty years ago. What will be the price next time?" The professed motives of war-makers, says Mr. Joad, are creditable; the real motives are not. The nation is a figment; there are only governments and peoples. The unavowed motives of war are mainly fear and pride. The effects on character are deplorable. Decent people talk and behave worse than wild beasts—who don't talk. "Every man who kills a German is performing a Christian act," said an English bishop. Can we be surprised that Lenin said to Mr. Lansbury, "Go home and convert the Christians"? A distinguished scholar wrote: Pacifists "are false as hell; they are like the outward appearance of the educated German. Those blue eyes seem to be full of candour; the ingratiating smile must please; yet behind them lurks the mind of a devil and the personal predilections of a herd of swine." As for the efficacy of war, is it not enough to say that we "drew the sword" in 1914 for three objects—to end war, to destroy German militarism, and to make the world safe for democracy? And the suffering and cruelty! Is it necessary to say anything about that—the mangled bodies, the broken hearts, the starvation and misery? "And what good came of it at last? said little Wilhelmine".

ROBINSON (*a historian*) Our sympathy with our friend Woolman was not diminished by the fact that, if I may say so, he got rather muddled at one point in his speech. It was the crux which has troubled Christian moralists for nearly two thousand years. Are we to allow, however reluctantly, a double standard of morality? Catholic theology has accepted the Stoic doctrine of a Law of Nature; but besides the absolute Law of Nature, which we may suppose works smoothly in Paradise, there is a relative Law of Nature, which must be accepted, as Woolman said, by beings "in a state of sin". The Church made great use of the words of Christ, "if thou wilt be perfect". Those who would be perfect must renounce life in the world with its necessary accommodations, and embrace what was called distinctively the "religious" life. The sects refused this concession. If the Sermon on the Mount was meant for some, it was meant for all. Christianity knows nothing of an honours school and a pass degree. But there is another possible compromise. Machiavelli, Hobbes, Bacon, Luther, and a whole bevy of German theologians and moralists have distinguished between public and private morality. The Sermon on the Mount should regulate our private lives; but the State is super-moral; it can do no wrong. If reasons of State require it, so Luther says, it may make wars; it may hang and behead men and break them on the wheel. This is a devilish doctrine, which is largely responsible for turning the modern world into a good imitation of hell. None of us here would accept it for a moment; but the fact that it has been seriously upheld proves that there is a real problem, which perhaps is most perplexing in the topic which we are discussing to-day. However, that is not to be the subject of my speech. I want to consider briefly whether history throws much light on the possibility of abolishing war.

We ought to begin, I suppose, with the animal creation. There is not much here that can be called war. The *cunnus, taeterrima belli causa,* leads only to single combats. Some animals, like wolves, hunt in packs, but not their own species. But Huxley is not quite correct in calling war a purely human phenomenon. Bee-keepers know what would happen if they left a piece of unclaimed honeycomb between two hives. Bees, no doubt, enjoy a much older civilisation than ours. They have arrived at a stable equilibrium, as perhaps we shall do some day. Some anthropologists have maintained that war is not really primitive. Man is so poorly provided with natural weapons that it was not till in the bronze age he acquired suitable killing tools that he adopted war as an institution. In Europe wars were almost continuous until Augustus established a unified Mediterranean empire. This is the solution which Napoleon offered to Europe, and which Hitler now offers—peace as the result of a knock-out blow by the strongest military Power. The evils of war are so great that even this kind of peace was welcomed, and Gibbon is not the only historian who has thought that the second century of the Roman empire was an unusually happy time. But the peace even then was frequently broken, and the outcome was the exhaustion, not the prosperity, of both rulers and ruled. At the present time, when the sentiment of nationhood and the love of independence are stronger than they have ever been before, the dream of a universal empire could hardly be realised, even if the conqueror were not the object of almost universal fear and hatred as Germany is. The Dark Ages reverted to barbarism in this as in other ways, and in modern times, under the newly consolidated nationalities, war became "the sport of kings". At this time the employment of mercenaries was general, and mercenaries, though prone to plunder and outrage upon civilians, do not wish inordinately either to kill or to be killed. Even in the wars of religion fighting was seldom internecine. In the eighteenth century there was a movement for humanising warfare, and hopes were entertained that war would in time be abolished altogether. The tide turned in the French revolution, when the French levée en masse signalled the emergence of the totalitarian State. Mirabeau, in 1790, tore up the nonsensical claim, so often repeated since, that democracies are more pacific and less unscrupulous than monarchies. "Voyez les peuples libres; c'est par des guerres plus ambitieuses, plus barbares qu'ils se sont toujours distingués. Voyez les assemblées politiques; c'est toujours sous le charme de la passion qu'elles ont décrété la guerre." By one stroke of baleful magic the French nation was transformed into a predatory horde. Of course the example was followed, and bettered, by Germany, though it was not till 1870 that it was applied completely. War thus became, for the first time, an intolerable curse. If it is not ended, and that soon, it will end civilisation. The accident that over forty years of peace followed Sedan prevented the world from realising at once the frightful danger it was in. The Great War gave Europe a shock which produced a serious though unhappily abortive movement for the abolition of war. The patient has had his second stroke. We shall not know for some time whether civilisation has received a mortal blow. The war will almost certainly be followed by chaos and civil troubles, as in Spain. France can hardly escape revolution, and there are menacing underground forces in Germany. We shall not be safe from revolution at home.

The great saying of Christ, that those who take the sword shall perish by the sword, has been verified again and again in history. Just as wolves and lions and tigers are at last exterminated as public nuisances, so wolf-nations sooner or later, and most often sooner, go to their doom. Assyria had a long innings, but there was nothing left of her when her enemies had done with her. The pugnacious Greek cantons really committed suicide. Rome tore herself to pieces; *"suis et ipsa Roma viribus ruit"*. Early food is late poison, says Bagehot. He who rides on a tiger can never dismount, says a Chinese proverb. When Andrew Marvell has done goading on Oliver Cromwell, who was by no means a megalomaniac, to be a Cæsar to Gaul and a Hannibal to Italy, he ends his fine poem with a rather ominous stanza:

"Besides the force it has to fright
The spirits of the shady night,
The same arts that did gain
A power must it maintain."

That is just it. It is not easy for a conqueror to convert his sword into a ploughshare. He must go on
using it. He has begun exploiting his victory, and he
must go on exploiting it. But a class or nation that lives
on plunder is doomed. It may die out, or be absorbed,
but the military virtues will not save it, for its victims
will be too apt pupils, and the love of freedom is
stronger than the habit of domination.

The age-long conflict between Europe and Asia
seemed, fifty years ago, to have ended in the decisive
victory of the West, which is inhabited by the most
pugnacious and acquisitive branch of the Hominidæ.
But the battle is not over yet. No civilisations have
been so stable as those of India and China, which have
certainly not been always pacific, but which, as compared with Europe, may be regarded as types of un-
military nations. The Vedas recognise war, and
Hinduism has a military caste, but the famous
Asoka wished to abolish war, and Buddhism is
radically pacifist. It goes further than any Christian
Church in condemning all forms of violence, but its
language is often strikingly like that of the New
Testament. "If you desire to honour Buddha," a
Brahmin is quoted as saying, "follow the example of
his patience and long-suffering. If you conquer your
foe by force, you increase his enmity; if you conquer
by love you will reap no after-sorrow". The temper of
Hinduism is also gentle, and the prosaic but sensible
ethics of Confucius honour the orderly, industrious,

respectable life. In China the soldier is not much respected; next to the scholar, the good citizen ranks highest. Thus two great nations have practised for thousands of years a comparatively peaceful un-aggressive life. It is only too probable that brutal Japanese aggression may force the Chinese to mili-tarise themselves; but on the whole they seem confident that they can hold their own without fighting against any foreigner, when once they have freed their country from the invader. Those who know them best have no doubt that they can.

A peaceable civilisation is therefore possible. It has been tried on a large scale, and has proved remarkably stable. If you want to survive, it is better to be a sheep than a wolf. But I am not at all sure that we in Europe will make this choice. The earth is strewn with the relics of dead civilisations, which have not died of old age. But if we are determined to perish like the Gadarene swine, it will not be for want of warning.

BATESON I don't want to make a speech, but I want to protest, not against anything that Woolman and Robinson have said, but about what they did not say. Of course we all know that war is wicked and unchristian; we don't need the Society of Friends to teach us that. And of course we all know that it is as foolish as it is wicked. But it is not our fault. It takes only one to make a quarrel, and it was certainly not we who made this quarrel. Our mistake was that we were so desperately anxious to keep out of war that we trusted the honour of one of the worst scoundrels who ever plagued humanity. There is no problem about it. Europe has been assaulted without provo-cation by an armed gangster. There are such people, unfortunately.

ROBINSON Perhaps I ought to have discussed the phenomenon of the super-brigand in history. But I did not want to make my speech too long, and you will remember the wording of the motion before us. I think we want to hear a psychologist next, and I hope Green will treat our subject from this side.

GREEN Our friend's protest illustrates one tendency which interests the psychologist, the love of personification in order to find heroes and villains. Bateson's devil is Herr Adolf Hitler, one of those adventurers who are always washed up to the top in revolutions. Hitler is no doubt a bad man, a bad man who has become worse under the influence of megalomania. As Lord Acton says, "Power always corrupts. Absolute power corrupts absolutely. So-called great men are almost always bad." Hitler is a transient phantom, though a very mischievous one. As soon as he fails he will be bundled out unceremoniously, and will vanish from the scene unwept, unhonoured, and unsung. That is the usual fate of deified adventurers. When Napoleon was beaten at Leipzig and obliged to leave France, he had to disguise himself as an English officer —Colonel Campbell he called himself. Otherwise he might have been lynched on his way to the coast. So savage tribes sometimes beat the images of their gods when anything goes wrong. We are rather good at furnishing our chief enemies with horns and a tail— Louis XIV, Napoleon, Nicholas I, William II, Hitler. But in investigating the psychological causes of war a more important part is played by the myth of national character. It is one of the most persistent and disastrous illusions in the world. We shall probably admit that the continental picture of our own countrymen is not only unfair but ridiculous. We are

63

perfidious, they say. In reality our governments never have deep-laid schemes, because under a democracy policy can be neither secret nor consistent. We have also an ideal of fair play, and as a rule we try to live up to it. We are a nation of shopkeepers, said Napoleon. We are rather bad shopkeepers, since we have neither the niggardliness of the French bourgeois nor the industry of the German. We are "proud and despise other nations". Ever since the Boer War we have been in a chastened frame of mind. Our critics contradict themselves freely. Which is true—that we take our pleasures sadly, as Froissart said (we are tired of hearing this), or another medieval line *"Anglia plena iocis, gens libera, digna iocari?"* The French think we are prone to suicide; our suicide rate is one of the lowest in Europe. A German in 1592 found the Londoners "magnificently apparelled"; Shakespeare about the same time laughs at our carelessness in dress. But enough of this. I have heard every quality attributed to my countrymen except meekness and loquacity; and, not to speak of Macaulay and Gladstone, we have all known some Englishmen and many English women who, as the saying is, could talk the hind leg off a donkey. Our judgments about the character of other nations are equally foolish. To take only our nearest neighbours, can we predict the conduct of anybody when we know that he is a Scot, or a Welshman, or an Irishman? Are we sure that even what we call the inferior races would differ much from ourselves if they lived under the same conditions? Darwin records that a Fuegian child who was educated in England developed a good intelligence and a nice disposition. I do not know whether he was surprised or not. Human beings are really very much alike, and, poor things,

64

they all want the same thing, to be able to live their lives in tolerable comfort and security. There are real differences among nations, of course, the result of climate, for instance. The want of energy among the inhabitants of sub-tropical countries may come from a moist enervating climate, or from such diseases as hookworm. In some of the South Sea Islands life may have been too safe and easy. But national hatred, based on supposed bad qualities pertaining to a nation as a whole, is quite unjustified. We sometimes think that all Prussians are bad Europeans, brutal, cruel, and war-loving. But that sound internationalist Kant was a Prussian; Nietzsche, Treitschke, Wagner, Houston Chamberlain, and Hitler were not Prussians. Our ideas of national character are formed partly from the actions of dominant personalities, like Palmerston or Bismarck; partly from the class which is dominant at this or that period—for instance, a feudal aristocracy will behave differently from an industrious middle class; and partly from traditional prejudices which may have no foundation at all. I do not think that anything would do more to cure the warlike temper than the extirpation of this pernicious illusion about national character. One might fill a volume with the arrant nonsense that has been talked by normally sensible people on this subject. We are no better than our neighbours in this habit.

In what follows it will be seen that I have been reading William Brown's book on the psychological causes of war. He is, however, a disciple of Freud, a prophet who leaves me quite unconvinced. The most fundamental of the forces which make war possible are, he thinks, the tendencies of self-preservation and self-assertion and aggressiveness, and the instincts of

65   E

acquisitiveness and pugnacity. Some degree of these tendencies or instincts is normal; but in war-time an abnormal state of mind prevails. The peoples wallow in emotion and in irrational hatred.* After the war there is a strong reaction. The majority of the demobilised soldiers in 1919 were resolved that if they could prevent it this should not occur again.† I am glad Professor Brown thinks that Chamberlain's visits to Munich were "a test and a challenge which in retrospect can be seen to have been invaluable in the knowledge they have brought us and the impression they have made on the whole world". Among other things, they showed up Hitler in his true light as a shameless liar. Besides this, Brown might have said that if we had gone to war for the Czechs we should have had to fight without France and without our Dominions. The enemies of the Prime Minister knew this, but they were—politicians. War and culture, Brown says, are incompatible. Its results are callous-

* "National hatred is something peculiar. You will find it strongest and most violent where there is the least degree of culture." *Goethe*.

† The following figures, from Professor Heering's book, *Die Zondeval van het Christendom* (1928), may be interesting. "A noteworthy phenomenon of recent years has been the growth of the Ponsonby movement in England and abroad. Lord Ponsonby, Under Secretary of State for Foreign Affairs, submitted to the Prime Minister a Peace Letter, signed by 128,770 British subjects, as follows: 'We, the undersigned, convinced that all disputes between nations are capable of settlement either by diplomatic negotiation or by arbitration, hereby solemnly declare that we shall not support or render war-services to any Government which resorts to arms'. So many more signatures came in that Lord Ponsonby decided to continue his effort. In the Rhineland and Westphalia alone, 137,000 men and women had signed by the end of 1927. In 1928, 135 Danish ministers declared, 'We should deem it an honour to our country if it were the first to accept disarmament'."

ness, and the general lowering of the moral tone. The regression in international conduct is a sequel to the Great War. When we remember the sudden outbreak of war-fever in August 1914, and the incredible things which were said and believed at that time, we must allow that there is such a thing as collective and contagious insanity, welling up from the unconscious part of our minds. In their sober moments the people of all countries desire peace. And yet at times a whole nation may exhibit signs of paranoia, imagining itself encircled by enemies. The result is megalomania and a ruthless desire for power. It is an uprush from the unconscious, which may be so violent as to carry off his feet the politician who stimulated it half sincerely for his own ends. The popular press at such periods has much to answer for. The remedy is not "an orgy of pacifist sentiment", but a psychological education, enabling the young to understand and to "sublimate" these anti-social tendencies and instincts. In this way a true League of all Nations may at last come into being. But it may be a long business. Mass psychology must be studied as well as individual psychology, and it is much more primitive. In war-time governments are only too successful in mobilising the unconscious. False propaganda is very wicked, but it is believed because in their abnormal condition people wish to believe it. Group mentality puts a premium on unconscious mental functioning. Swift makes God say, "I damn such fools!" The psychologist will feel more pity than indignation. Brown says: "I cannot conceive a more terrible situation in international affairs than that in which an aggressive and ambitious paranoiac, firmly and fanatically entrenched in his delusional system, should achieve leadership of a powerful and

67

LIBRARY
WAYNE STATE COLLEGE
WAYNE, NEBRASKA

warlike nation and infect his immediate subordinates with an aggressive paranoid tendency aiming at world-domination. Let us hope that this situation will never arise." It did arise only a few months after these words were written; or perhaps we may say it was already in existence. We are going through a period of retrogression in political affairs which may or may not lead to a partial or total collapse of our civilisation. But if we can learn something about the workings of the human mind—and there are some already who could teach our rulers if they were willing to listen— the disaster may be averted. Sooner or later, but I fear not sooner, war will be abolished. We are told that we cannot change human nature. Perhaps not; but we can change human behaviour.

I am therefore doubtful whether I could support the motion, though I have left no doubt about my sympathies. Those who are now living will hardly see the end of the "blatant beast". But it is possible that I may be wrong. Experience is a good teacher, though her fees are terribly high.* I quite agree with Woolman that if we were all Christians nearly all our social troubles would be over; but the Founder of our religion was not encouraging to those who dream democratically that the larger crowd will ever be found on the narrow way. Something less than the heroic standard of the Sermon on the Mount should be enough to bring this insanity to an end. We need not call in the saint or the philosopher, but only Aristotle's *phronimos*, the sensible, right-thinking, decent fellow who remembers his own dignity and the rights of his neighbour, *dignitatis suae et libertatis*

* "Eventu rerum stulti didicere magistro," says Claudian, after Livy: "eventus stultorum magister".

alienae memor, as Livy says—no bad definition of a gentleman.

MORDAUNT   I yield to no one in my admiration for the Quakers. They have the courage of their convictions, and many of them are the salt of the earth. But as for pacifists in general, I don't like them. When I hear some of them quoting Johnson's unfortunate saying that patriotism is the last refuge of a scoundrel (which he did not mean in that sense at all), I say to myself that they are the kind of people whom I should like to drive to their last refuge, and that I would help them into their funkhole with a good kick on the pants. Some of these gentry obviously pride themselves on their superiority to patriotism and loyalty. One of them gracefully describes the enthusiasm at the Coronation as "bally-hoo". Why, they say, should people pretend to be excited over a ceremony like that? Loyalty is simply unintelligible to them. And what is patriotism but "an absurd prejudice founded on extended selfishness"—Ruskin's words, unfortunately. "A virtue among barbarians," says Havelock Ellis. I wonder whether they are equally superior and detached about the merits of their wives, children, and friends. Herbert Spencer speaks of an anti-patriotic bias; and some of these people seem really to hate England. Every enemy of this country has his champions among us. The English, it would seem, differ from other misguided rascals in never being in the right even by accident. These people were much surprised that wage-earners, whom they absurdly call proletarians, put their country before their class when the call to arms sounded. They were annoyed that class bitterness almost ceased while the country was in danger. For few of them are really pacifists; it is only disinterested

69

loyalty that they object to. In my opinion, our country deserves the love and admiration of its citizens; and though we have occasionally gone to war unjustly, our aims have generally been to protect the liberties of ourselves and other nations against the ambition of some aggressive Power. Is Freedom not so precious a possession as to deserve that great sacrifices be made to preserve it? For my part, the words of our orators and writers on this subject move me to the heart. I have copied out two or three of them. Burke said: "As long as you have the wisdom to keep the sovereign authority of this country as the sanctuary of liberty, the sacred temple consecrated to our common faith, wherever the sons of England worship freedom they will turn their faces towards you. Slavery they can have everywhere; it is a weed that grows in every soil. They may have it from Spain; they may have it from Prussia. But until you become lost to all feeling of your true interest and your natural dignity, freedom they can have from none but you". Is not this the literal truth to-day? Are we not still stirred by the funeral oration which Thucydides puts into the mouth of Pericles, and by the famous Gettysburg speech of Abraham Lincoln? Do we not think that to die for liberty is a martyr's death? Is it for nothing that some of the noblest poetry in the world has been inspired by the heroism of the soldier, and by faith in the poet's own country? I do not defend the bombastic speech of Henry V before Agincourt, in Shakespeare; but I hope we are not unmoved when we read—

This England never did, nor never shall,
Lie at the proud foot of a conqueror.
Come the three corners of the world in arms,

And we shall shock them. Nought shall make us rue,
If England to itself do rest but true.

Much of our best patriotic poetry is founded on an
intense affection for some part of our island home.
There is no nation, I think, in which this emotion is so
strong as with us. Sir Walter Scott celebrates the love
of the Scot for Caledonia, stern and wild; Yeats that
of an Irishman for Ireland. Wordsworth, Matthew
Arnold, Hardy, and many more have dwelt lovingly
on English country scenes; none more poignantly than
some of the victims of the Great War, such as Rupert
Brooke, Sorley, and Grenfell. Most assuredly those who
so love their country are ready to defend it with their
hearts' blood. I do not think that any condemnation
of war is satisfactory which does not take into account
the appeal that it makes to heroic hearts, to that eager-
ness for self-sacrifice which is a strange but most real
part of a man's make-up. There are things which any
decent man would die rather than do; and there are
things which any decent man would die rather than
suffer. As long as this is so, and as long as powerful
nations are liable to epidemics of aggressive militarism,
I do not see how war, and preparations for war, can be
done away with. It is not fair to compare war with
savage customs which we have outgrown. There is
much more in it than that, including a disinterested,
if sometimes quixotic, desire to stop injustice and
tyranny in countries with which we have no treaties or
close relations. "Curse ye Meroz, said the angel of
the Lord; curse ye bitterly the inhabitants thereof;
because they came not to the help of the Lord, to the
help of the Lord against the mighty." It was said by a
foreigner that in diplomacy our actions are unpre-

dictable, because we, unlike other nations, are capable of going to war for an idea. I think it is true, and I am glad that it is.

WOOLMAN I am glad we have had one apologia, not for war but for the soldier. What Mordaunt has said wanted saying. Heaven forbid that we should say anything that sounds ungrateful to the young men who are risking their lives for us, or that we should suggest that those who have fallen in the service of their country have died in vain. It is just the appeal which war makes to many noble natures which has kept a horrible institution in being for so long. And yet how great is the detestation which has been felt for it for thousands of years! Even in the Iliad, which is entirely devoted to deeds of arms, Zeus tells Ares the war-god that he is hateful to him above all the other dwellers in Olympus. The great soldiers have often loathed their trade. "If you had seen one day of actual war," said Wellington, "you would pray God that you might never see another." "War is hell," said the American general Sherman. This is rather different from Napoleon's remark, "What do the lives of a million men matter to me?" And yet I suppose more books have been written about Napoleon than about any other figure in modern history. Is it not time that we ceased to honour the successful brigand who "wades through slaughter to a throne, and shuts the gates of mercy on mankind"? I doubt if any man has ever caused so much unnecessary misery to his fellow-creatures as Adolf Hitler. He is not even a great soldier; his ambitions are as barbarous and outmoded as those of Genghiz Khan and Timour. He and all that he stands for are a hideous anachronism. I have not attempted to indicate how war can be abolished;

but I still maintain, after all that has been said, that its abolition is the most pressing task of civilisation, and that if it is deferred much longer our civilisation will dissolve in chaos and unimaginable horrors.

IDEALS AND IDOLS

SPEAKERS: *Inge (82), a Victorian fossil; Sparks (50), a moderate Labour M.P.; Titmuss (30), a British Fascist.*

SPARKS Well, Dean, are there any idols still left on their pedestals?

INGE I undeaned myself eight years ago; I am only a Doctor, or rather seven Doctors.

SPARKS I thought once a Dean always a Dean.

INGE That applies only to Bishops, organs of the Holy Ghost, as one of them told us the other day.

SPARKS What happens when Their Infallibilities disagree, as I suppose they do sometimes?

INGE Then, as Selden says about Church Councils, the odd man is the Holy Ghost.

SPARKS Well, everyone calls you Dean, so you must put up with it. But I want to have a talk. You are, I think, a Diehard?

INGE Not a Live-easy, certainly.

SPARKS But you are a strong Conservative?

INGE I don't know what Conservatism means now. I once gave a lecture at Ashridge, and found them all Socialists. When I remonstrated, they said they must float with the tide. I told them that any dead dog could do that, and that I agreed with Lowell:

> "He's a slave that would not be
> In the right with two or three."

SPARKS Splendid! But who are the other two?

74

INGE   Three people can keep a secret, if two of them are dead.

SPARKS   So you are the only survivor—the last Whig, shall we say?

INGE   Perhaps; the Devil was the first, according to Dr. Johnson.

SPARKS   It is not like the Devil to be in a minority of one. He favours the big battalions.

INGE   Yes, he captures them, but he lets them fight under their old flag. Labels are always libels.

SPARKS   Well, we shall agree in wanting to send Titmuss here to prison. He is a Fascist, perhaps a Nazi. He has a new flag; it looks like a Christian emblem a good deal battered.

INGE   We won't call in the police, Titmuss. But will you tell us why you are a Fascist?

TITMUSS   I will if you like.

INGE   Do you approve of persecuting the Jews?

TITMUSS   I dislike them, but I don't want to maltreat them.

INGE   Do you approve of killing people without trial; of torturing them in concentration camps; of mutilating them? Do you approve of the total extinction of every kind of liberty; of the barbarising of a once civilised country; of the systematic poisoning of the minds of the young by mendacious propaganda? Do you approve of fanatical State-worship; of unprovoked aggression upon weak neighbouring States; of brutal militarism and shameless acts of violence and cruelty?

TITMUSS   I don't justify all that the dictators have done. But revolutions are not made with kid gloves. Look at what the Reds have done in Russia and in Spain.

75

INGE I do look at it, with horror. But why are you on the side of the assassins?

TITMUSS Because they are not merely assassins. Our people use "Fascism" or "Nazism" as swear-words, without attaching any definite meaning to them. They talk of Hitlerism, and point out with glee that Hitler is not at all a great man, but the boss of a team of gangsters. They seem to think that if Hitler were hanged or assassinated the Germans would give no more trouble. Hitler is an astute adventurer, who has risen to the top in very peculiar circumstances. That is more or less true of all leaders of revolutions. Even Napoleon said "I could not replace myself", and he had the sense to say, "If I disappeared, what would the world say? They would say 'Ouf', with infinite relief". But you ought to realise that it is just because he is not a great man that he is so profoundly significant. You old and middle-aged people do not understand—how should you?—the spirit that is blowing like a whirlwind through the youth of Europe. Only a breath of it has come to England as yet, though there is more of it than you think. It is a spirit of radical revolution, of rebellion against all the ideas of the nineteenth century, a spirit of contempt for all the fetishes before which our fathers and grandfathers used to bow down. We have no more use for Conservatism, Liberalism, Democracy, Communism, Monarchism, Liberty, Science, Philosophy, Humanism and Humanitarianism, Moralism, Christianity. All of them must go.

SPARKS A fairly comprehensive spring cleaning! You are anti-everything. And when you have made a clean sweep of our civilisation, with the help of an army of clean sweeps in black shirts, what do you propose to put in its place?

76

Titmuss   We do not know. We have no programme. We do not think; we will and act. Some great and noble order of society will come to birth as the result of our ardent faith and hope. What it will be we do not know, but it will be something entirely different from anything that the world has seen hitherto.

Sparks   It seems then that your activities are purely destructive, your aims absolutely vague.

Titmuss   Destruction must come before reconstruction.

Sparks   Unfortunately for the world, the aims of the totalitarian States are not in the least vague or negative. At the back of all this claptrap about a New Order is something which is not new at all, something primitive, barbarous and savage. An insane and perverted romanticism has taken the form of dreams of world-conquest. I have not got my books here, or I could prove to you what mad schemes are propounded in all seriousness by Germany, Italy, and Japan. At present they propose to divide the world among them, like Octavius, Antony and Lepidus; but Germany and Japan both boast so loudly that we may doubt whether one planet is large enough for both. There has been nothing so monstrous since Attila, Genghiz Khan and Timour, who spread ruin and destruction over Asia and part of Europe. It is useless to palliate this undisguised aggressiveness. No nation ever threatened any of these countries. Europe was united in the desire for peace and disarmament. The misery which this wickedness has brought upon the world is absolutely incalculable. Not to speak of the flower of two generations cut off prematurely by senseless slaughter in these two wars, we of the Left had visions of a number of large schemes to better the lot of the poorer classes, all of which could have been carried out generously at an expense to the taxpayer of less than one-twentieth of what these two wars have cost. We could have abolished poverty and placed the advantages of education and refined enjoyment within the reach of all, without destroying the comforts of the middle class culture which I, at any rate, have no wish to disparage. Now the upper and middle classes, with the traditions which gave a character to our civilisation, are completely ruined, and the chief source from which our social services were supplied is permanently dried up. Civilisation has been thrown back fifty years if there are no more wars; if the present insanity continues, there may be another Dark Age lasting for centuries.

TITMUSS I will not interrupt you, Sparks, but as an Englishman I am naturally not in favour of aggressive imperialism.

SPARKS But, my dear man, that is an integral part of Fascism. Do you suppose that the very nebulous "revolution" which you speak of would induce whole nations to shout "Guns, not butter"?

TITMUSS I will answer you presently; you have not finished.

SPARKS Well, consider the arguments by which aggression is justified. There is the claim to *Lebensraum*, which has some plausibility in the case of Japan, not much in the case of Italy, and none at all in the case of Germany, which is not nearly so thickly populated as England or Belgium, and where the population, even under artificial stimulation, will soon become stationary. If we are to admit, which I do not, that a nation with an unregulated birth-rate has a right to expand at the expense of its neighbours, it is the Slav, not the Teuton, who will need to stretch his legs. Russia will have 250 million inhabitants before Germany has 100 million. Then there is the absurd theory that the Germans, as a Nordic race, are the predestined and rightful rulers of the world. This utterly unscientific theory, which is derided by all ethnologists, has been so often exposed that I need say no more about it. Thirdly, there is the worship of the God-State, which is supposed to be above all considerations of right and wrong. But you, Dean, have dealt faithfully with these pestilent doctrines in more than one of your books.

INGE I have; and since our friend here does not seem anxious to defend that side of Fascism, we may take this part of our indictment as read. But there is one aspect of the question on which I should like to say a few words. Why has this frenzied nationalism broken out in these three nations, Germany, Italy, and Japan? For it is not a universal phenomenon at all. We have seen that some large empires have broken up in consequence of provincial agitations for independence —Austro-Hungary and the British Empire are the most prominent examples. It may be part of the same tendency that violent hatreds exist between neighbouring peoples, as we see above all in the Balkans. But rampant militarism and aggressiveness are almost confined to the three nations which I have mentioned.

SPARKS We shall be glad to hear your views on this point.

INGE Well, as regards Japan I am afraid we brought our troubles upon ourselves. We bullied the Japanese when they only wanted to be left alone. If we had not interfered with them, they might still be an artistic feudal society, fighting among themselves with two-handed swords, or even with bows and arrows. But we observe that the two European countries, Italy and Germany, were the last to achieve unity. Italy, after a brilliant period of independent city States, recalling the flowering-time of Greek civilisation, was still divided into provinces, and had long been oppressed under foreign rulers. Spain, Austria and France had all inflicted wounds upon Italian self-respect. As for Germany, it was like a jig-saw puzzle. It was repeatedly invaded by foreign armies, and was devastated—half depopulated—in the Thirty Years War. Under the small State system it had become the spiritual home of philosophers, musicians and scholars; but it was the cockpit of mercenary armies.

SPARKS Are you not forgetting Frederick the Great and his father? Were not they very modern Prussians?

INGE Frederick played the eighteenth-century "game of kings" more astutely and rather more unscrupulously than even his rivals. But no better Europeans and anti-militarists ever lived than Kant, a Prussian, and Goethe. (I am told that the young Nazis have never heard of Goethe, and cannot spell his name.) It was Napoleon whose criminal ambition to conquer the world called into activity the dormant spirit of militant nationalism. In Prussia, whom he treated worst of all, the sleeping demon came out roaring. Consider how, ever since Jena, France and Prussia have alternately belaboured each other, not at all for their souls' health, like a pair of Flagellant monks. And each time the flogged has had his revenge on the flogger. Nothing can illustrate better the folly of militarism. If China, the most peaceable country in the world, goaded to desperation by Japan, should militarise itself, what will be the consequence to Japan, and perhaps to Europe?

SPARKS I agree with all that you have said about Germany and Italy; but the age-long rivalry between Europe and Asia is a bigger question than even the struggle between Slav and Teuton. I think we had better leave Japan on one side to-day.

INGE Very well. I think it is time to hear what Titmuss has to say for himself and his disreputable clients.

TITMUSS What I said just now about the revolutionary whirlwind which is sweeping over the younger generation on the continent of Europe must, I know, have seemed to both of you pure insanity. If you cannot believe that such a frame of mind exists, I advise you to read what men who know Germany from the inside, Rauschning for example, have said. It is, of course, an apocalyptic vision, and apocalypses always sound absurd. But these visions control events, though not always in the manner which the visionaries expect. Did not Christianity begin with dreams of a new heaven and a new earth? But of course I know that the directors of totalitarian politics are not dreamers of this sort. English publicists do not seem to understand the conditions on the Continent. Mussolini, who began as a revolutionary, realised that he had to choose between Fascism and Communism, and he chose the former. Liberalism is dead, and Democracy is dead; the choice was between class war and militant patriotism. That is not so in England. Here we are witnessing the emergence of a new privileged class— organised labour. This is not a victory of the proletariat; there is no proletariat here; the Trade Unions represent the lowest stratum of the bourgeoisie, who

F

are far too well off to want revolution; besides, except where their pockets are concerned, they are conservative and conventional. But in Italy and Germany the conditions were quite different. I know it is often said that Communism was no longer a menace in Italy in 1922. I disagree; the country was torn to pieces by industrial strife; there were political strikes and a great deal of violence. In Germany, where the Communists had lately polled six or seven million votes in the year before Hitler seized power, popular government had been wrecked by the refusal of the Communists to co-operate with the Social Democrats. The Communists wanted revolution; the Social Democrats wanted radical reform.

SPARKS Very good, Titmuss; but you are not a German or an Italian. Why are you a Fascist?

TITMUSS I will come to that presently. The dictators decided to bring the class war to an end by putting the State in the place of the Party as the object of loyalty and devotion. Were they right or wrong? It was a bold stroke, for they could not know which ideal would prove the stronger. The revolutionaries of the Left put up a poor fight; though there was a lot of street fighting —more than we in England realise. Those who know Germany think that there are not many Communists or Social Democrats left. Whether that is true it is hard to say, but for the time they are crushed and silenced.

INGE And do you think that the dictators chose the better part, as well as the stronger side?

TITMUSS Yes, I do. Contrast Germany and England now, when the two countries are at war. Here we have a Conservative majority in Parliament, but the Government is in manifest terror of a revolt of the workers. We are told that the war costs thirteen millions a day. Does anyone suppose that it need cost anything like that? Half of it goes either in blackmail, exorbitant wages paid to men who think that their country's difficulty is their opportunity, or in slack work, or in wanton waste, which seems to give a peculiar pleasure to the beggar on horseback. But I suppose you, Sparks, will say that there is not a word of truth in this.

SPARKS There is more truth in it than I should care to admit publicly. But it would be very unfair to bring a charge of want of patriotism against the working class in this country.

TITMUSS I do not wish to do so. It is just a matter of comparison. The German worker works for longer hours and lower wages than in England, and, above all, he pays from 15 to 20 per cent of his income in taxes. If our Government suggested anything of that kind there would be a general strike at once.

SPARKS The German workman cannot help himself. He may end by revolting.

TITMUSS I don't know what he will do after the war, but there are no signs of it at present. "All for Germany" is enough for him now. And consider another thing. In the totalitarian countries it is a coveted honour to belong to the Party. In the democracies politics is a dirty business, and politicians are not trusted. This is less true with us, where an older tradition still exists; but in France a politician is generally suspected of being something of a crook.

SPARKS We will hold our inquest on poor Democracy presently. But I differ from you entirely when you think that the people of Germany are happy and contented. After all, they are of the same flesh and blood as ourselves. And is it conceivable that any government should pursue a policy of sheer terrorism, universal spying, and organised mendacity unless it is secretly afraid? And why have the chief gangsters invested seven million pounds of their stolen property—a capital offence, by the way—abroad, unless they know that they will probably have to bolt sometime?

INGE   I agree with you. It is well established that Himmler told Hitler that in the event of war he must have 250,000 soldiers to keep order in Germany.

TITMUSS   In my opinion the Nazis have made themselves absolutely safe. A rebellion against a totalitarian government is impossible.

SPARKS   Unless the army turns against them, and the army is full of the fanatical young Nazis whom you described to us. What do you think will be the end of Hitlerism, Dean, if, as seems to me probable, it survives this war?

INGE   I think the gangsters will throw themselves more and more into the hands of the army. A military dictatorship is the natural outcome.

SPARKS   What difference will that make?

INGE   I think Hitler will liquidate Himmler and his Gestapo. It would be a very popular move, and with the army behind him he will no longer need them.

SPARKS   Himmler might get his fist in first.

INGE   That is quite possible.

SPARKS   Would the military dictatorship try to conquer the world?

INGE   I think not. The soldiers will have had enough of fighting.

SPARKS   One thinks of what they call prætorianism in the Roman Empire. In the third century the army set up one emperor after another, and then murdered him.

INGE   The parallel is not close, because the Roman

84

army then consisted mainly of barbarian mercenaries. The German army is young Germany.

SPARKS Then you don't think Hitlerism will be overthrown by a rising of the masses, the army refusing to fire upon them?

INGE The difficulty is that there is at present no alternative to Hitler. Communism is dead, abandoned in Russia except for export. Marx and his philosophy belong to the economist period of political science; they are now quite out of date. And if the German people do not want Communism, what do they want? Titmuss was right in saying that they have no use for parliamentary Liberalism. They don't want the Hohenzollerns. They are more than ever afraid of civil war now that, as they must be aware, they are universally, intensely and justly hated as no nation in history has ever been. What remains for them except to put up with Hitler?

SPARKS There is one other possibility. The gangsters may destroy each other. That is how revolutions generally end.

INGE Well, these are speculations. Let us hear what Titmuss has to say about Democracy. Perhaps I shall agree with him this time.

TITMUSS The notion that the ballot-box is a Urim and Thummim for ascertaining the divine will or for securing political wisdom is really too absurd for argument. It seems to be assumed in the United States, but in that country Democracy is a blessed word which may mean anything or nothing. We are very busy offering lumps of sugar to the American eagle, but I doubt whether many Englishmen honestly think that as an experiment in government—and that is all that Democracy is—it has been a great success. The Great

War, which was to make the world safe for Democracy, has convinced the whole world, except in the English-speaking countries, that Democracy is not safe for itself. Can anyone say that universal suffrage brings the right men to the top? Are democratic politicians respected or trusted anywhere? Have they not debauched the citizenship of the working man? Is not this country now divided into two nations—not the rich and the poor, as Disraeli said in the novel with a title which he could not spell, but the taxpayers and the taxeaters? What has become of the old constitutional maxim, "No taxation without representation"? Democracy breaks up society into atoms and collects them again into mobs, and what the majority want is *panem et circenses*—the dole and the dogs.

SPARKS I think all this is too unfair. Compare the condition of England a hundred years ago with what it is now. The masses then were rough, brutal and dirty. Many of them were half starved. Democracy has brought them out of the house of bondage; it has made England a civilised country, instead of a country with a civilised upper crust. But I suppose, Dean, you agree with Titmuss?

INGE I think what you have just said is quite true.

SPARKS You sometimes speak as if you did not think so.

INGE I am afraid I do. I lose my temper. The court chaplains of King Demos, who have the impertinence to call their own brand of sloppy Socialism Christian economics, make me sick. Perhaps the best thing to be said about Democracy is that it is a good educator. But granting that it has been a useful instrument for abolishing or diminishing admitted social maladjustments, is it not possible that it is essentially destructive, not constructive, and that it has done its work in clearing the ground? That, I think, is what Titmuss is really driving at.

TITMUSS   Yes, it is. There is a whole mass of lateral reforms which parliamentary Democracy has never touched and never will. There is one thing which the democratic politician never forgets—that the unborn have no votes. I think you, Dean, are a keen member of the Eugenics Society?

INGE   I used to be, until they took up this silly depopulation stunt, and family allowances, the effect of which would of course be to sterilise still further the class which would have to pay for them, the class into which the pick of the wage-earners are being artificially drafted by government grants. We are creating a class of Babus, educated proletarians, for whom there is no room in the professions, the parlour Bolsheviks of Bloomsbury.

TITMUSS   Well, the Fascists are determined to make the next generation physically fit. I don't like mutilating people against their will, but the intention is good—that future generations shall be sound in body. Travellers in Germany speak enthusiastically about the fine appearance of the youths and maidens as they march in procession, or work—as every young German has to do for so many months—in the fields. Seventy-five per cent of the young Germans who were tested for military service were passed in the first class.

SPARKS   That is good, but we might have that without Fascism.

TITMUSS   We might, but we don't. Then think of unemployment. There is no unemployment in Germany.

SPARKS   There is no unemployment in Dartmoor prison.

87

TITMUSS And the abolition of class war. The organisers of the general strike of 1926 would have been shot in Germany for high treason, and a good thing too.

SPARKS That is not our way of doing things. Our methods may fail—they would fail against a fanatical or uncompromising revolt; but the democratic countries hope to avoid such fierce antagonisms.

TITMUSS They may, by mass bribery, as long as the loot lasts.

SPARKS Come, Titmuss, the British working-man is not a cadger or a parasite.

TITMUSS No, but he is out for what he can get out of what he calls the State.

INGE There are two very important questions on which we have not yet touched, and on which I think Titmuss may make out a case for his clients. It is plain, of course, that Sovietism and Fascism are becoming more like each other every year. We may call the system planned economy or State capitalism.

TITMUSS That is the essential thing, the main out-come of the revolution. Extreme nationalism may be only a passing phase.

INGE Then let me say what I think about it. When I was a young man the Fabians were talking about a planned society. It was not very attractive. I did not like regarding myself as only an item in a census return, to please the Sidney Webbs. But during the Great War, and still more during the present war, we were and are a planned society with a vengeance. After the war, nearly everybody thinks, we must have a great deal more planning. But what shall we plan for? A just and peaceable order of society, or an efficient machine for aggressive war? I am afraid, in spite of

Titmuss, that all Fascist planning is quite openly and avowedly of the second type. It may be a passing phase, but it is certainly not an extraneous or non-essential feature at present. And if only one great Power organises itself in this way, must not its neighbours do the same in self-protection? The defence of Democracy against Fascism, says Aldous Huxley, entails inevitably the transformation of Democracy into Fascism. Such are the accursed results of militarism even in one country. There is no doubt that experiments in planning will be tried. They must be on a national, not on an international basis; and they will certainly interfere with international trade, which worked smoothly enough before planning was thought of. Each nation will try to make itself economically independent of its neighbours—a most reactionary idea. In over-populated countries like ours this would be quite impossible. It is also inevitable that the officials in charge of the plans will make many mistakes. Finally, under State capitalism everyone's livelihood would be at the mercy of the bureaucracy. There would be less liberty even than we have now. I therefore do not look forward to planning with any enthusiasm. My other subject is the question what will be the substitute for Democracy? Here we may get more help by studying Italy than Germany. The corporative State of Mussolini seems to me the one important innovation of Fascism which we may do well to consider. The essence of it is that the nation shall be divided occupationally and not locally, and that each profession or trade shall manage its own affairs. Here Mussolini admittedly borrowed much from Sorel the Syndicalist, but whereas Sorel advocated class war and violence, Mussolini has arranged that in every administrative board employers and employed shall sit together. I do not know how this plan has worked, but it seems to me far superior to parliamentary Democracy.

TITMUSS This is more than I hoped for. You have virtually admitted that, whether you like it or not, Fascism must come, and further, that one of its main experiments, the corporative State, is worthy of consideration by the democracies.

SPARKS I think we will now ask the Dean to sum up our debate. He is not quite such a hopeless old reactionary as I thought, and he will be more merciful to Titmuss and his friends than I should be.

INGE I will begin by a confession. Delisle Burns in his book about Democracy was pleased to say that a playwright (Bernard Shaw) and a Dean (myself) would like to govern the country themselves. A pretty pair we should have been! Well, if I had been dictator I should have kept the country out of both wars. I understand from a Cabinet Minister who was present that at the fateful meeting of the Cabinet at the beginning of August, 1914, the majority were in favour of neutrality, till Asquith frightened them by saying that if we did not help France we should be left without a friend in the world, and that the French would hate us more than the Germans. We might have to fight them both. But I also heard that certain powerful influences at the Foreign Office were strongly pro-French and anti-German. Well, the French alliance has not done us or them much good. Paradoxically, the chief beneficiaries of the allied victory were the Russians, whose country we saved from dismemberment. I cannot help thinking that a nation which has everything to lose and nothing to gain ought to reflect twice and three times before staking its all on a gambler's throw. I have also always thought that if we had kept clear of the French entanglement we could have made a deal with Hitler. I formed this opinion not only from *Mein Kampf*, in which I believe Hitler for once spoke his real mind, but from the writings of some foreign publicists, including Gunther, the clever and well-informed author of *Inside Europe*. Of course, neutrality would have meant non-interference on the Continent; but we are frankly not in a position to police Europe, and our well-meant interpositions have done nothing but harm to our protégés. Abstention would no doubt have been dangerous, and it is quite possible that the mirage of world-conquest has disordered the ill-balanced mind of Adolf Hitler as it did the much colder and more lucid mind of Napoleon. In that case we should have had to fight sooner or later. However, I still think that South Russia is his main objective. But it is useless to raise this question now, and in any case the Japanese have left us no choice.

These two wars are the greatest calamity that has ever befallen the human race. I agree with all that Sparks has said about that. But whereas the guilt of the Great War should not have been entirely laid upon Germany—the revelations of Franco-Russian preparations made known by the Bolsheviks are not pleasant reading—the Germans really have no case in the present war. The French after the Revolution of 1789 honestly wished to bring liberty, equality and fraternity to nations which knew none of them. But the Germans have no wish to infect other nations with their ideas. Nothing could be more inconvenient to them. Their New Order means simply domination for

91

themselves and serfdom for the rest of the world. Beyond this they have no clear idea what the New Order means. This was plain enough from what Titmuss has said.

He drew us a picture of what I can only call pannihilism, a repudiation of everything that men have believed, hoped and valued for two thousand years and more. This attitude I frankly cannot understand. The slogans of the nineteenth century no longer appeal to us; that I realise. The economic man of the half-century after the Napoleonic war begat twin brats— acquisitive Capitalism and acquisitive Socialism, who loved each other like Cain and Abel. Both of them are out of date; the quarrel between them is like the question between crinoline and hobble skirt. The belief in a law (not a fact) of progress is also dead. It was a secularised apocalyptic, a pale reflection of religious belief. The future, as Anatole France says, is a convenient place to store our dreams; but why should the loss of this dream bother us so much? Above all, why should these disillusionments take the form of hideous cruelty? The number of cold-blooded murders ordered by Hitler himself is quite appalling, and recalls the massacres of senators by half-insane Roman emperors. How many perished in the blood-bath of June 30th, 1934, will never be known. H. A. L. Fisher thinks that about 1,200 were murdered; 250 is another and more moderate estimate. I have long suspected that among his victims was von Hoesch, the German Ambassador in London. The Ambassador was dining with us on July 24th, 1934—it was the last dinner-party that we gave at the Deanery. He was looking very well and told us that his doctor had given him a clean bill of health. A few days or weeks afterwards—

I forget the exact date—we heard that he was dead; and two other diplomats died with suspicious suddenness in the same week. But one would like to know why, in certain countries only, do we see the emergence of a new type of young man, enthusiastic and self-denying in some ways, but utterly brutal and callous? He has been described many times; he is to be met with in Germany, in Italy, in Russia, perhaps in Spain. But we have no young Nazis here. I fear Titmuss would forfeit his deposit if he stood for Parliament in any constituency.

Some have said that these new developments are the result of despair. But what was there, before this war, to despair about? The common man was better off than at any other period of history. Technology had filled the world with the materials of comfort. Was the world such a bad place? Personally I have found it pleasant enough, and if I had not sometimes worried myself over troubles most of which never came, I should have had a very happy life.

As a Christian and a Platonist I should say that people are unhappy when they lose their faith in the eternal spiritual world. They lose their moorings and drift aimlessly. But this after all is only a symptom. Why has faith become dim in our time? I sometimes think that we do not allow enough for the aftermath of the Great War. The upset may not be so complete or so lasting as we suppose. But alas! the second war will aggravate every dangerous symptom. For no good can ever come out of war. The wrath of man worketh not the righteousness of God.

SPARKS   Thank you, Dean. You have owned yourself puzzled, and, good heavens, so am I. But I find that there are still a few remarks that I should like to

93

make. I have been reading Rauschning's new book, *Makers of Destruction*, which consists of conversations with a great many representative Germans in the years between 1933 and 1939. Almost all of them insist that Germany is in the midst of a tremendous revolution, something much bigger than Hitlerism and destined to survive the present team of gangsters. Some of them mean by revolution the pannihilism of which Titmuss spoke with approval. And it is worth mentioning that this doctrine is older than Hitler. It appears full-fledged in Spengler's famous book, which had such an amazing success in the 'twenties. On his last page Spengler, after predicting an era of "Cæsarism", in which the "culture" of modern times will decline into a disintegrating "civilisation", ends by saying that those nations which "prefer truth and justice to deeds and the will to power" must go down; such antiquated notions have no survival value. He has said earlier in the book that nations which are beginning to decline —a process which is ordained by fate, so that it is useless to resist it—expand and make wars of conquest. Such is the destiny reserved for Germany in the present century. I was surprised to find this theory half accepted by Arnold Toynbee: as far as I know, it is not confirmed by history. Whether this advocacy of "Cæsarism" and immoralism is due to Spengler I do not know; many Germans certainly regarded him as a prophet. Beyond this, Rauschning's friends were extremely vague about the revolution. The smaller States of Europe are to be absorbed into one large group, dominated by Germany. According to some of them, Nationalism and State-worship are to be things of the past. The small nations will not resent the loss of their independence, since everything will be arranged for their comfort. The Greater Germany will extend from the Seine to the Urals. Britain will be left out in the cold, though if Iceland and Greenland like to join us Germany will not object. All this is characteristic of a nation which with all its great gifts is politically immature. But why all this talk about the tremendous revolution? It is not peculiar to Germany. The Baltic Baron Count Keyserling writes a book called *La Révolution Mondiale;* the Austrian Drucker *The End of Economic Man;* the Russian Berdyaeff *The End of the Age.* There seems to have been almost unanimity on the Continent, before the second World War, that Europe was in a state of revolution. And yet we in the English-speaking countries are not conscious of anything of the kind. (I am not thinking of the changes which may follow the present war.) I represent a Labour constituency, and there are social changes which I support; but none of us wants to upset the coach; we leave subversive schemes to the young intellectuals of Bloomsbury. There is one Communist in the House of Commons—a harmless individual—and not one Fascist. How and when did revolutionism on the Continent begin? When the Great War ended, the mass of the people wanted to go back to the peace, plenty, and liberties which they had been denied during the four years of fighting. There were disturbances in most countries, but except in Russia they were easily suppressed. The general strike in England fizzled out. America flourished wondrously under Coolidge. The French, after suffering severely from inflation, settled down quietly in 1926. In Russia Stalin overthrew Trotsky, and substituted State capitalism for Communism. Even the Germans had a trade revival, financed most unwisely by foreign loans. But one very

95

notable new phenomenon was coming to light. Bolshevism was a proletarian revolution, directed not only
against the upper and middle classes but against
organised labour. The Bolsheviks abused the trade
unions quite as savagely as the bourgeoisie; they
destroyed the German republic and played into Hitler's
hands by their violent hostility to the German Social
Democrats. It was the despised "little man" who made
the German revolution, and the drive came mainly
from the lower middle class, completely ruined by
inflation, rather than from organised labour, which
was protected to some extent by social services. The
technique of the new revolutionaries was far superior
to that of the Marxists, entangled in outmoded
economism. But it was not till the economic crisis of
1929 that revolution seemed to be imminent. This
crash revealed the incompatibility of political economic nationalism and an actual international economy. This was often represented as the downfall of
capitalism. Many of my socialist friends hold this view.
In my opinion it was rather the *reductio ad absurdum*
of nationalist "autarky"—really a preparation for war
—in a world where uncompromising nationalism
contradicts the actual state of society. So great was
the danger of war that very soon a militarised form
of State socialism was set up in one great nation
after another. The great Society which had partly
established itself, as Sir Arthur Salter says, "more like
the structures built by the instincts of beavers or ants
than the deliberately designed works of man," was
torn to pieces by the parochial fears and jealousies of
nations, and with it perished, for a time, the comity
of European civilisation. Disillusioned and terrified,
the continental nations surrendered their liberty to

any organised power which promised to defend them. We, as an American visitor said, were "the only people in Europe who are not scared". Perhaps we ought to have been scared. Elsewhere, law and order collapsed, and private armies were collected, a thing unheard of since the middle ages. We have been made to see what a planned social order involves. If a multitude is to be subject to a plan, it must be militarised. If individuals are allowed a free choice the plan is thrown into confusion. Bureaucracy under an absolute ruler or rulers is necessary. Popular assent can be secured only by rigorous censorship and prohibition of free discussion. Espionage is a necessary part of the system, and a considerable amount of terrorism. Since private expenditure must be controlled it is wise to keep private incomes near a subsistence level and to dole out any surplus on collective pleasures such as free holidays. The system works most easily in times of scarcity, and especially during a war; where the consumer is master, regulation is more difficult. We shall not understand totalitarian tyranny unless we realise that it is the result of planned economy; it is a lesson which we have yet to learn. Another danger which we politicians of the Left perhaps realise more clearly than we dare to say is that democratic governments are often at the mercy of self-regarding pressure groups, who regard "the State" as a milch cow. In France this has disgusted thinking men with Democracy. Every representative is thought to have been sent to Paris to "get something" for his constituents. You see that I am being very honest; we all have to think seriously why what Fisher calls the great Liberal experiment is now so much out of favour. But I have not yet explained why there is in many continental countries this belief

97   G

in a total revolution. I really cannot explain it; I am puzzled, as the Dean confessed that he is. No doubt historians will explain it all to our descendants. "The whole," says Saint Beuve, "acquires after the event a deceptive semblance of reason." All that I see is that a secularist religion is trying to propagate itself with a ferocity peculiar to religious fanaticism. And I would add that much as I detest the dualism of Lutheran ethics—the double standard of public and private morality—the present absorption of private in public morals, the repudiation of all the values hitherto accepted by all civilised men, is not really in accordance with the German character and tradition. I think it is too monstrous to last. Forgive me for this long disquisition, after I had in a manner closed the debate. I never meant to talk so much.

THE DISMAL
SCIENCE

SPEAKERS: *Two Oxford Dons — Popham, a political economist; Hudson, a historian; and Inge, a rustic moralist.*
TIME: *The spring of 1942.*

HUDSON   Are you disposed for a long walk? I want to talk shop.

POPHAM   Right you are. Your shop, or my shop?

HUDSON   They overlap, that is the worst of it, and in the near future they threaten to coincide.

POPHAM   You historians are no good at predicting the future. You always favour the gods against Cato, and back the winner after the event.

HUDSON   Economists are just as bad.* We both try to be up to date, and there is nothing so reactionary as being up to date.

POPHAM   That remark is worthy of old Inge. Shall we look him up at Brightwell? He knows nothing about political economy, and not much about history, but he thinks for himself and is not always wrong. It is a pleasant twelve-mile walk by Clifton Hampden, and when Mrs. Inge has given us tea we can come back by bus from Wallingford, or by train from Didcot.

HUDSON   By all means. You say historians are bad prophets. But have you ever thought of collecting the

* "S'il existait une monarchie de granit, il suffirait les idéalités des économistes pour la réduire en poudre." *Napoleon.*

predictions of distinguished statesmen and public men? Men of letters are not infallible, but they compare very favourably with politicians. Here are a few examples; I have them in my pocket, I thought they would amuse you. I include one man of science, since they fancy themselves just now. Shelburne: "When the American colonies gain their independence, the sun of England will set, and her glories be eclipsed for ever". Washington in 1786: "The age of conquest has ceased". Sir Humphry Davy: "It would be as easy to bring down a bit of the moon as to light London with gas". Pitt in 1792: "There never was a time when one might more reasonably expect fifteen years of peace". Bismarck: "Russia can never join France against Germany". Nelson: "Neither Malta nor the Cape will ever be of any importance to Great Britain". Winckelmann in 1768: "In fifty years there will be at Rome neither Pope nor priest". William Wilberforce: "I dare not marry; the future is so unsettled". Shaftesbury in 1848: "Nothing can save the British Empire from shipwreck". Disraeli in 1847: "In industry, commerce and agriculture there is no hope". Wellington in 1852: "I thank God I shall be spared from seeing the consummation of ruin that is gathering about us". Fox said in 1803 that a war with France would "effect the total destruction of the influence of this country on the Continent". Wellington in 1832: "Few people will be sanguine enough to imagine that we shall ever again be as prosperous as we have been". Gladstone in 1863: "Mr. Jefferson Davis has made an army, he has made a navy, and more than that, he has made a nation". In the summer of 1870 a Cabinet Minister said in Parliament that he saw no clouds which threatened peace in Europe. Arthur Young, Heine,

George Meredith and Matthew Arnold saw what was coming much better.

POPHAM Yes, and most of the men whom you have quoted were prophets of evil, which is consoling. Well, I have been reading again two rather disquieting books, Drucker's famous *The End of Economic Man* and C. H. Pearson's *National Life and Character*. The latter is fifty years old, but he was very much alive to the Yellow Peril. I suppose the book is still in demand, for I found eight copies of it side by side in the London Library, where they complain of being cramped for space. But I want to talk about Drucker first. I was not quite so much pleased with his book after reading it the second time.

HUDSON Why not?

POPHAM It may be prejudice. The end of economic man would, I suppose, be the end of teachers of political economy. Othello's occupation would be gone.

HUDSON But you must be used to hearing your subject abused. Carlyle and Ruskin wielded effective bludgeons. And now every whippersnapper orates about that monstrous abortion, the economic man, without heart or guts, who actually supposed that men were guided by reason, and that pleasure and pain can be measured or weighed like packets of sugar.

POPHAM Yes, I am quite used to it; but Drucker is modern, and carries rather heavy guns.

HUDSON What in his book does not please you, on the second reading?

POPHAM To begin with, he harps upon "equality", which he couples with freedom. But who cares about equality, except the Irishman who said, "One man's as good as another, and a deal better too"? Freedom, yes, we want that; and security, we want that badly; but equality—the factitious equality of unequals, we don't care about that, at least in England. In France perhaps they do,* and in America they believe in fraternity; but liberty is enough for us. And why does Drucker call a chapter "The Despair of the Masses"? Do the masses despair? Not here, at any rate. Why should they? Democracy, Socialism and Communism are discredited, as Drucker says, but our working-class does not know that they are discredited, and never believed in them much. Organised Labour is far from despairing. If any class has a right to despair, it is that to which you and I have the misfortune to belong. We had our golden age in the last century; now we have nothing but poverty to look forward to, though I hope not the utter ruin which overtook the professional class in Germany in 1923. But I don't think even we despair. If we still know our Horace, as I fear we don't, we should say of Fortune:

> "Laudo manentem; si celeres quatit
> Pennas, resigno quae dedit et mea
> Virtute me involvo, probamque
> Pauperiem sine dote quaero."

Are things so very different in Germany and Italy? Are the people, as Drucker says, utterly disillusioned and despondent, ready to welcome the new totalitarian gospel just because it is purely destructive and negative? I think some continental publicists—Keyser-

* "France will be socialistic and communistic before it will be able to establish a liberal republic, because equality is infinitely easier to establish than liberty. The International and the Ultramontanes aim equally at dictatorship." *Amiel* in 1870.

ling is another example—leave the English-speaking nations too much out of account. After all, we fill a not insignificant place in the world.

HUDSON   Rauschning speaks of a world-revolution now in progress.

POPHAM   Yes, but this is not "despair" at all. Revolutions never come from despair. They always occur with a rising market. Aspiration, not desperation.

HUDSON   Then how do you account for the revolution in Germany?

POPHAM   I think I should name three causes, not at all as an exhaustive enumeration. First, and perhaps most decisive, was the impatience of a proud and militaristic nation at a tame, "bourgeois", pacific policy. Germany was bored with Weimar, as Paris in 1848 was bored with Louis Philippe.

HUDSON   I agree so far. No nation can stand being well governed for long.

POPHAM   My second reason is their contempt for parliamentary Democracy, a sentiment which is almost universal except among Anglo-Saxons. My third is one which Drucker, an extreme radical, fails to appreciate. He thinks that the German masses were disappointed with Russian Communism. The fact is that the German people were in deadly fear of Russian Communism. Our Left-wing apologists try to make out that Communism was not a danger either in Germany or Italy. But those two nations had seen it at uncomfortably close quarters. There is much information about this in Arthur Bryant's *Unfinished Victory*. Drucker in the same way quite misunderstands the situation in Spain; he thinks the interposition of Germany and Italy on the side of the Nationalists was merely a Fascist plot. It was much more. They were afraid of a Bolshevik government in the west of Europe, helped by France. The Reds, under the tutelage of Krivitsky, had taken complete control of the Spanish government, and had committed hideous atrocities. The official estimate is that 300,000 harmless people were butchered at Madrid, Barcelona, and other places. The Warden of New College told Inge that when his brother, Admiral Fisher, visited Barcelona, the British Consul called upon him dressed like a workman. "If I ventured into the streets dressed like a gentleman," he said, "I should be murdered." This is just to show that even Drucker is not free from political prejudice.

HUDSON   I am sure you are right. But Germany was quite as much afraid of Russia as of Bolshevism. German officers were uneasy about the new spirit in the Russian army, and a more serious menace loomed in the near future from the Russian birth-rate.

POPHAM   Our friend whom we are going to see was much complimented on his prediction that Hitler and Stalin, who had been abusing each other like a pair of bargees, would soon make an alliance, as they did shortly afterwards. I suppose both were playing for time.

HUDSON   There was a real conflict of policies in Germany. Hitler and Rosenberg were convinced that Russia was Germany's real enemy, and that the conquest of the Ukraine was the most profitable field of expansion. Ribbentrop, infuriated by the social snubs he received in London, where he was nicknamed Brickendrop, wished at all costs to destroy Britain. To a historian it is interesting to compare Napoleon and Hitler. I think Napoleon regarded England as his one irreconcilable enemy. He attacked Russia because he could not allow any leak in his blockade of our island. No doubt Hitler's European conquests have the same motive; but until lately he always thought a deal with England possible, while the conflict between Teuton and Slav must be fought to a finish.

POPHAM   Germany's fear of Russia is reasonable; the fear of Bolshevism is not.

HUDSON   That was not so clear ten years ago, when Hitler came into power; still less twenty years ago, when Mussolini marched on Rome. Besides, though Russia has renounced Communism, it is still useful for export, to make mischief abroad. Very many Germans think that if Hitler falls, there will be a Communist revolution in Germany.

POPHAM   Well, this is not the part of Drucker's book which I most wished to talk about. In the nineteenth century, he says, economism was taken for granted. A good government was one which promoted the greatest possible increase in the aggregate wealth of the nation, and a good social system was one under which prosperity advanced "by leaps and bounds". This optimism of the Victorians fell out of favour when our golden age of expansion came to an end. The business career no longer offers many prizes; our young people nearly all play for safety, which often means some little job under Government. From the worldly point of view it was well worth while to make a fortune in the nineteenth century; now it is not, since taxation makes it impossible to "found a family", and the country-house life of the leisured class, even if it were possible, would be found boring by most of our young people. But I want to discuss what Drucker says about Germany under Hitler. It is rather puzzling, because what little economics there is in *Mein Kampf* is all in favour of free competition and non-interference by the Government.

HUDSON Hitler is an opportunist, like all careerists. He was brought into power by several divergent groups, each of which thought it could use him and then turn him down. So far, he has been too artful for all of them. Thyssen, for instance, financed him at first, and then found himself thrown aside. When he remonstrated with Hitler, the Führer said that he ought to be thankful to be allowed to keep his head on his shoulders. The pressure of the Socialists has pushed Hitler further to the Left, and this means that he has discarded his earlier economist theories.

POPHAM According to Drucker, his great achievement is to substitute non-economic for economic rewards and satisfactions, for determining a man's position in society. Nazism is a social revolution but not socialist; it retains the industrial system, but in fetters. It offers the workers, not more money, but concert tickets, foreign trips, and other "symbols of social position". These leisure-time organisations have a very beneficial effect in diminishing social dissatisfaction with economic inequality. The Nazis go further. They divide society into economic "estates" which have a recognised and honourable place in the social structure. The peasants, for example, may be an economic liability, since small farms do not pay, but the peasant is styled "the biological backbone of the nation". The urban worker is "the spiritual backbone", the middle class "the standard-bearer of national culture".

HUDSON There is not much culture in Germany now, except the National Socialist variety.

POPHAM There is the further advantage that all

classes are fused together in the various semi-military organisations. It is said that these have a social and political rather than a military object, for the army chiefs do not believe in huge armies of imperfectly trained men.

HUDSON That is why Roehm and his Storm Troopers were liquidated. They were not wanted, and they were credited with radical views.

POPHAM Prussian Junker Society was never plutocratic, but undoubtedly class distinctions were strongly marked.

HUDSON I understand that the richer classes are very heavily mulcted, which no doubt partly reconciles the workers to total loss of the powers which the Trade Unions exercise in other countries. The Government will not allow any independent organisations to retain any vestige of freedom; the learned professions, for example, are muzzled and degraded.

POPHAM But here we come to a feature which interests me very much as an economist. You know the American theory of "consumptionism". Raise wages so that every employee can purchase lavishly; organise mass production of everything that he wants, and supply and demand will play merrily into each other's hands. The example always quoted is the huge Ford works at Detroit, where wages are very high and profits enormous. Of course this is because everybody wants motor-cars; if Ford made grand pianos or anything else for which there is only a small demand, the system would not work. I never have believed in consumptionism. The system in Germany is managed consumption; the German view is that depressions are caused by over-consumption and under-investment. Accordingly there is a vast amount of compulsory saving. We are now following the same course. In both countries the propertied classes are being proletarianised; for the compulsory savings of the German are not allowed to do much good to the investor. But it is said that more than half of the national income is being "saved".

HUDSON Is not this purely a war measure? In peace-time would not under-consumption strangle industry?

POPHAM The German answer to that is very instructive. The productivity of German industry is enormously greater than can be absorbed by home consumption. Therefore the surplus must be unloaded on the foreigner. Europe is to be divided into three zones. In the West, Great Britain, which may perhaps be joined by Denmark, Iceland, and Norway. In the East, part of Russia. The whole of the rest of Europe, including the Ukraine, is to be an economic bloc controlled from Berlin. The existing independent nations are to manage their own internal affairs, but otherwise they will be satellites of the German Reich. This, they say, is just and reasonable, because the Germans are a superior race, destined to rule over the "lesser breeds". They require a higher standard of living; more food, for example. The function of the dependent nations will be chiefly to supply Germany with food and raw materials; but they will also consume German manufactures. Germany will be industrialised from end to end, and will be enormously prosperous. What do you think of that programme, Hudson, as a practical proposition?

HUDSON I do not think it is practicable. Nothing is more evident than that the desire for complete independence on the part of societies which consider themselves nations is stronger now than at any previous time. A nation has been defined as a group of persons united by a common error as to their origin, and a common hatred of their neighbours. A very absurd sentiment, perhaps; but it exists almost universally. It was not strong at the time of the French Revolution, and the French were at first welcomed as deliverers in the countries which they invaded. But Napoleon awoke the dormant spirit of nationalism, which has never slept since his fall. Is it conceivable that the nations of Europe will submit tamely to domination from Berlin? Our friend at Brightwell told me of an interesting conversation which he had with Professor Hans Delbrück, the well-known publicist, at Berlin in 1912. In answer to an expression of regret at the ill-feeling between the two nations, Delbrück said, "I don't think ill-feeling matters much; but where there is fear there is danger". Where there is fear reinforced by indignation at oppression and injustice—for other nations will not readily admit that the German, being a superior being, requires more comfort—is it not certain that Germany will be the object of such universal, intense and just hatred as has never before been felt against any nation? *Oderint dum metuant*, "let them hate me provided they fear me", Caligula used to say; an abominable sentiment, Seneca thought. Abominable or not, it necessitates continual watchfulness and tyranny; and these are expensive. Besides, the Germans are not indifferent to the judgment of other peoples; they know that they are not loved, and cannot understand why. The Germans look forward to settling and trading in the conquered countries. This will not be easy for them. As for economic prosperity, the inferior races will not have much money to buy German goods, and they cannot be prevented from manufacturing some of them for themselves, more cheaply. The plan of industrialising Germany from end to end is quite contrary to German policy in the past, and is not approved by the whole party. To maintain the importance and dignity of agriculture is part of the party programme. Many of the Nazis wish at all costs to avoid the mistake which we made when by repealing the Corn Laws we ensured the ultimate ruin of British farming. The peasantry are everywhere a stabilising influence. Workmen collected in large towns are always a danger to the established order; and experience shows that they cannot be kept contented by high wages. Lastly, the whole conception of *Lebensraum* is based on a romantic error. The Germans increase very slowly; their country is not over-populated; and the countries which they covet are either already full or are being rapidly filled by much more prolific peoples. The whole scheme, though worked out on paper with German thoroughness, seems to me just a piece of perverted romanticism.

POPHAM I think you are right. And yet Arnold Toynbee, and others too, have been convinced that the present system of independent States, arming in terror of each other, cannot continue, and that a "knock-out blow", delivered by the strongest of them, may be the way out. Augustus established a sort of peace in the countries round the Mediterranean.

HUDSON The Roman Empire ended in the suicide of the conquering Power. It is one possible end to our troubles, but I do not think Europe would put up with it for long. Think of the vitality of venomous animosity in Poland, Ireland and Bohemia, and the failure of Austria and Turkey to hold together a "ramshackle empire".

POPHAM Before we leave Drucker, and come to the other book which has disturbed my equanimity, I want to consider the next chapter in his book, which he calls "Miracle or Magic". We have done half our walk. What a charming village Clifton Hampden is with its bridge over the river. Oxfordshire and Berkshire have lovely villages, and this is one of the best.

HUDSON Is Nazism a miracle or a mirage?

POPHAM Unless war is accepted as an end in itself, Fascism has not solved the problem of class-war and inequality. That is what Drucker says. He makes too much of the fetish of equality, but it is in the name of aggressive nationalism that internal conflicts have been suppressed. War is glorified as the supreme expression of heroic, self-sacrificing man. But this ideal does not appeal to the masses, who regard it as senseless. The masses in the totalitarian countries hate war. They showed it by the demonstrations which greeted Neville Chamberlain at Munich, and (according to Drucker) by the sympathy shown to Schussnigg just before the invasion of Austria. If this is true it is very important. The Nazis have been obliged to invent "demons" on whom to throw the blame for their militarism, and these demons are frankly incredible to any sensible man. In one breath the Nazis glorify war and profess their devotion to peace. The British Government are denounced as "war-mongers". The Czechs were preparing to bomb Berlin. "Der Karnickel hat angefangen"; "C'est le lapin qui a commencé"; "Cet animal est très méchant; quand on l'attaque il se défend." But the poor animals did not even defend themselves. The persecution of personified demons has become almost the whole of the Nazi creed; it justifies brutality, violence and deception. Anti-semitism is the most complete form of this persecution. It was hoped that it would be popular, since the successful Jew is a very annoying person, and the unsuccessful Jew is often a Bolshevik. But the average German, who is not a savage and is fairly intelligent, sees through the deception and is disgusted with the cruelty. In the hope of conciliating the masses, Hitler has declared war against the bourgeoisie, personified as the Jew. In fighting the Church the Nazis are combating the love of peace and the ideal of an international order. More and more, organisation becomes an end to itself, and therefore any real organism must be suppressed. Drucker might have mentioned the persecutions of the Christians under the Roman Empire, which had a similar motive. But all these things are signs of weakness, not of strength. The mirage will dissolve as soon as it becomes possible to restore freedom and self-respect to the individual.

HUDSON I agree that all this violence and humbug are signs of weakness; but history shows that autocracies live long and die hard. So long as the choice is between tyranny and anarchy, people will usually put up with tyranny, if tyranny is efficient.

POPHAM Well, now for Pearson's book. He is obsessed with the Yellow Peril, though it is China, not Japan, that he is afraid of. Perhaps he will prove right in the long run. The sentences in which he sums up are as impressive as they are pessimistic. It is more than probable, he says, that the time is approaching when what we call the lower races will predominate in the world, and when we shall ask nothing from the day but to live, nor from the future but that we may not deteriorate. It seems to me, as a student of political economy, that the greatest of all questions is whether the future belongs to the high-standard or to the low-standard nations. I ought, I know, to have a clear opinion about it, but I have not. The future will decide one way or the other.

HUDSON I have friends on the Right wing of politics who think that political pressure by the trade unions is killing our foreign trade and creating unemployment. They have called my attention to a book by Professor A. L. Bowley, who is certainly not prejudiced against Labour. Among the causes of the slump in foreign trade and the increase of unemployment he mentions "the forcing up and maintaining of wages at a level not warranted by the economic situation, which has been rendered more possible by the unemployment insurance scheme". It is notorious that there are tens of thousands of men who are able and willing to work but who cannot earn trade union wages. The unions have decided that they must not work at all.

POPHAM Some of our Left-wing economists say that the evil is under-consumption. They point to the destruction of coffee and other comestibles which, it is alleged, cannot be sold, although many people want them. It is the same argument which Carlyle used a hundred years ago. I do not say that I agree with it.

HUDSON But now about the competition of cheap foreign labour. The people of California, British Columbia, and Australia are convinced that if the Chinese or Japanese were allowed to settle in their countries the white man would soon be squeezed out. In plain language, the yellow man gives much better value for his wages.

POPHAM   Yes; and that is not the whole story. Why do we allow swarms of low-grade Irish, most undesirable citizens from every point of view, to come to Glasgow, Liverpool, and other places? Why do the French admit millions—I think millions in the plural —of foreigners of all sorts, from Belgians to Senegalese? Why are many villages and towns in New England almost deserted by the old American families and filled with Italians and French Canadians? Why are Mexicans allowed to settle in Texas? Why can South Africa never become a white man's country? Why are the hated Poles tolerated in Prussia? The answer is everywhere the same. Cheap labour is wanted for rough manual work, which the privileged labourer will not do. This is nowhere more apparent than in France, where it is complained that even the racial stock is being contaminated. Nothing fails like success. A ruling race always rules itself out. Shall we say with Hannibal, "I recognise the doom of Carthage"?

HUDSON   Inge told me that shortly before he left London he had a call from a Japanese gentleman. The Jap began: "I hear that you have a strong belief in the League of Nations?" "I don't know about a strong belief. I began with faith and went on with hope; now there is nothing left but charity. But I certainly think that some agreement of the kind is the only hope for Europe." "We are not Europeans. If we disarm and join the League, shall we be allowed to settle in countries where there is plenty of room for us, and where we can work and bring prosperity—in Australia, for example, and California?" "No, I am afraid you won't." "We shall be kept out by force, as we are now?" "I am afraid you will." "Then why should we disarm and join the League?" It was not easy to find an answer.

POPHAM I hate to have to say it, but the Japs really have a case against us, as long as we keep our Dominions half empty. But might not an Australian say that the southern part of his continent is not empty, and that the northern part, where it is not desert, is too hot either for English or for Japanese? Theodore Roosevelt, who was fond of giving good advice, said, "Why don't you invite Italians to settle in Queensland?"

HUDSON I think Pearson over-estimates the handicap of climate. Townsville in Queensland has a climate like that of Bengal; but it is a fairly healthy town inhabited by people of our race.

POPHAM Then do you think that either we or the Japanese could colonise Borneo or New Guinea?

HUDSON No; the equatorial climate would not suit either of us. The Japanese, in point of fact, seem to be less adaptable to extremes of climate than the Chinese. Manchuria is too cold for them; Singapore is perhaps too hot; but the Chinese do very well in both. There are, or were, several Chinese millionaires at Singapore; and an English traveller in Manchuria found the first-class carriages full of Chinese, but the porter who carried his bag was a Russian. But the Japs could settle in Australia.

POPHAM Yes, the Chinaman can outwork and undersell the Jap; his standard is even lower.

HUDSON There is a very interesting chapter about Japan in one of Lothrop Stoddard's books. The Japanese, he says, are a mixture of Malays, Mongols, and Caucasian Ainus. I doubt, however, whether they did mix much with our distant cousins the "hairy" Ainus, who were and are savages. In any case, long isolation has evolved a stabilised racial stock. In the middle ages there was a long conflict between Chinese ideas and Japanese sentiment, which resulted in a militant feudalism, much like that of medieval Europe. Then in the sixteenth century Europeans arrived. The Japanese became as eager to assimilate European ideas as they had been to imitate the Chinese under the great Han dynasty. Catholic priests made many thousands of converts. Japanese merchants traded all over the Far East; their pirates annoyed the Dutch of Java. They crossed the Pacific to the Mexican port of Acapulco, and might easily have occupied the whole Pacific coast of North America. But again they revolted against foreign influences. When the Japanese Christians appealed for help to the King of Spain, that was the last straw. The Shogun massacred and at last exterminated the adherents of the Western religion. Japan was to be hermetically sealed against foreign intrusion. No one was allowed to leave or enter the country on pain of death, and all the larger ships were destroyed. Just a few Dutch merchants were allowed to trade at one port under humiliating conditions. The Japanese, says Stoddard, had made one of the supreme renunciations of history. It was successful, for the country enjoyed prolonged peace and developed a peculiar and rather beautiful civilisation.

Popham   I wish to goodness we had left them alone!

Hudson   I wish we had. We have no reason to be proud of the bullying behaviour of England and America which forced the Japanese to westernise themselves again. But perhaps the frenzied nationalism of Europe would have infected them anyhow. They have really outdone the Germans in chauvinism. "The expansion of Japan throughout the world and the elevation of the entire world into the land of the gods is the urgent business of the present." So one of them shouts, and there are many who use the same language. It is pure Nazism; they have no more respect for West Europe and North America than the Germans; they want nothing less than universal conquest.

POPHAM   Then they will have to fight the Germans. "When Hun meets Hun . . ." Your excursion into Japanese history has been very interesting; but our subject just now is economic competition. Is it as serious as some make out?

HUDSON   I think it is. Japanese stockings have been sold, at Manchester of all places, at threepence a pair. A French textile manufacturer exclaimed, "If I stole my raw materials and paid my workmen nothing I could not compete with such prices".

POPHAM   But I hear that the evils of unrestricted capitalism are rampant in Japan, and that the workers are ready for revolt. There are two gigantic capitalist firms, the Mitsuis and Mitsubishis, who dominate the economic life of the country, and control the parliament. They are so hated that they have to be guarded.

HUDSON   No doubt something will have to be done for the workers. But they have such an enormous lead that they can afford to make considerable concessions and still undersell the white man with a great deal to spare. How Lancashire is to maintain its trade with India I do not see.

POPHAM   Neither do I. Protection would be countered by exclusion of Indian cotton and Australian wool.

HUDSON   Besides, the wants of the Japanese workman are very modest indeed; and he is fanatically, religiously patriotic. Also, the rural parts of Japan are grossly over-populated and the cultivators are in abject poverty. There cannot be much difficulty in recruiting cheap labour for the factories.

POPHAM   The pressure of over-population may not be permanent. I suppose they know something of birth-control.

HUDSON   The net increase is still very large. But of course it cannot go on. Either birth-control or famine will stabilise population at the saturation point. But there is another possibility—successful war and mass emigration.

POPHAM   Heaven forbid! The idea of losing Australia is intolerable. .

HUDSON   But not entirely impossible. Fascist Japan is almost as formidable as Germany.

POPHAM   And when will the British working-man learn that he has no longer a prescriptive right to higher wages for shorter hours than the German or Italian, not to say than the Asiatic?

HUDSON   When the last goose that lays the golden eggs has had her neck wrung.

POPHAM   But here we are at Brightwell. This is the house. Did you ever see anything much more beautiful than the weeping willow in the middle of the pool, with its cascade of delicate green leaves? It suggests a Chinese landscape.

HUDSON   And here is the old ex-Dean, who has long ago discarded his apron and gaiters, pottering about his garden.

INGE   I am very glad to see you. Have you really walked all the way from Oxford?

POPHAM   Yes, talking shop the whole way. We thought we would look you up, in the hope that you might have something cheerful to say to us.

INGE Well, in spite of the *Daily Mail*, I never prophesied anything so bad as what has happened to the world. But you have paid me too high a compliment. I am not an economist. I suppose Mill, whom I used to read, is out of date, and the Fabians never convinced me. But don't talk to me about currency and inflation; I am quite out of my depth there.

HUDSON Nevertheless, you may have something to say. Bertrand Russell remarked once: "Plato, if he could return to this world, would make friends with Dean Inge, and accept his views on modern civilisation *in toto*". And Plato, I take it, was a totalitarian who disbelieved in liberty and hated democracy.

INGE There was one thing that he hated more— tyranny or dictatorship. Nietzsche said that he was a Christian before Christ, and I once said that he was a Hildebrandian before Hildebrand. But his Nocturnal Council was intended for atheists, Epicureans, and— Catholics.

HUDSON But let us know what you think about what people call the World Crisis and the New Order.

INGE We have got to get rid of the disorder first. As old Thomas Fuller says, that man will catch a bad cold who has no clothes except the skin of a bear not yet killed.

POPHAM Yes, first catch your *Herr* . . .

HUDSON But now fire away; we are listening.

INGE Well, I should begin by saying that the discrepancy between prices and real values is one cause of our social troubles.

POPHAM What do you mean by real values? Are not all values created by persons?

INGE I say certainly not. Some values are ultimate, intrinsic, absolute. These have no price, not being exchangeable for anything. They are, if I may say so, the thoughts of God.

HUDSON And are they revealed to us infallibly?

INGE In a sense, of course not. If I ask with Pontius Pilate, What is truth?, we may debate about the answer a long time. But if I know, or think I know, what is truth, and say Why should I believe it? there is no answer except Because you must. The pragmatists deny this, but I cannot argue with them now. It is just the same about right and wrong, and about the beautiful and the ugly. If I know what is right, I must do it; if I know what is beautiful, I must admire it.

POPHAM Economics, however, are concerned with relative or instrumental values.

INGE Yes; but do they not "participate", as Plato would say, in the absolute values, in very different degrees? All valuation implies a standard, and a scale of higher and lower. Sometimes, of course, the judgment is almost inappreciable, but I think one might maintain that there is no perception without valuation, which is perhaps important if true.

POPHAM And you say that a true valuation would make a very odd price list.

INGE It would indeed. Those instrumental values which have the greatest share in the ultimate values are increased, not diminished, by sharing them. I am thinking of all spiritual and intellectual values. I need not expatiate; I am sure you agree with me.

HUDSON In general, yes. But who is to be your valuer? Some would say the saint, who might be a poor judge of the beautiful, and unworldly not from knowledge of the world but from ignorance of it. Plato would say the philosopher; but he reminds us that Thales fell into a well, and was laughed at by a pretty Thracian maidservant. Aristotle would say any right-minded sensible man, a *phronimos*.

INGE   Well, we will be content with the judgment of the *phronimos*, subject to an occasional appeal to one of the other two.

HUDSON   And what would he say?

INGE   He would say that we may be and probably shall be deprived of a great many things which now command very high prices, the loss of which will not really make us any poorer. We don't really want large houses and a great many servants. Tobacco and alcohol have a small value if they give us pleasure, but we should soon cease to miss them. If women are ever sufficiently educated to be emancipated from each other, they will agree that pearls and diamonds are worth only a few shillings, since sham ones look just as well. As for cosmetics, they have a negative value, making a pretty woman look repulsive—to my eyes at least. But here I must admit that *de gustibus*—and *disgustibus—non est disputandum*. Hitler issued a decree against cosmetics, but the women were too strong for him; the German Fraülein has begun to paint her face again. But there are other negative values about which there can hardly be two opinions. Anyone who fosters envy, hatred, malice, and uncharitableness is impoverishing his fellow-men. I shall never forget a little speech made by Montagu James, then Provost of King's, at a dinner given in honour of the Vice-Provost, Fred Whitting, one of those dons who are greatly loved in their own colleges and not much known outside. "A man," he said, "who devotes himself to helping his colleagues to think better of each other does a greater service in such a society as ours than can easily be estimated."

HUDSON Popham and I would cordially agree there.

INGE Nothing more banal and commonplace than what I have been saying can be imagined. You will be sorry that you took the trouble to walk twelve miles. But our notions of value—I mean instrumental value—are so conventional that it is worth while to consider whether we really care about some things as much as we suppose. If we examined ourselves in this way, a good deal of unthinking acquisitiveness and ignoble envy might be avoided.

POPHAM What is your remedy? More education?

INGE Better education, and the best part of education begins when we have left school and university behind. Great subjects like philosophy and politics, as Aristotle says, are not suited to the young, who have had no experience of life. But, above all, religion—the right sort. I know that, as Whitehead says, religion may be a bad thing.

HUDSON I am glad you have not said that our generation is more materialistic and less spiritually minded than the middle ages. That is what we are always being told, and I don't believe it. Superstition is one thing, spirituality is another.

INGE Like you, I am tired of this claptrap. Money had much greater prizes to offer in the nineteenth century than in the middle ages, and therefore it was more sought after. But the Victorians were not more materialistic than the medievals. Nevertheless, I should like to call attention to some figures in the chapter on "Play" in Beard's book, *Whither Mankind.* The estimated annual "cost of play" in the United States was twenty-one thousand million dollars, which is not far from the aggregate income of Great Britain. In the "boxing *indu͞try*" Dempsey received 750,000 dollars for thirty minutes' "work", his opponent Tunney 450,000. The spectators paid two million dollars for their seats. There seems to be some discrepancy between price and value here.

POPHAM   Well, good-bye, rustic moralist, and thank you for giving us tea. It is a rum world, as I think someone has said before.

ON A COLLEGE
ESSAY

Luncheon at the Master's Lodgings, St. Jude's College. Present: the Master; his brother Chambers, a clergyman; Tresham, Tutor of the College; Richards, M.D.

MASTER Well, Tresham, how are you getting on with the Fellowship papers? Are they a good lot?

TRESHAM Yes, Master, there are some interesting men among them. I was working at the essays all yesterday.

MASTER What were the subjects?

TRESHAM We gave them the choice of three. "La propriété c'est le vol." "Art for Art's sake." "The Ethics of Suicide." Only two chose the second. Five took the first. The other ten wrote on suicide; most of them justified it.

MASTER Were the five Communists?

TRESHAM I shall not give our candidates a title in a foreign language again. It puts us in difficulties. Three of the candidates wrote rather conventional essays on collectivism. One of the others, a pessimistic moralist, lamented that "Propriety is on the wing"— which it certainly is, but that is not exactly what Proudhon meant. The fifth, a scholar of Balliol, wrote a really original essay on "Personality consists in Volition". What are we to do with him?

MASTER I should be merciful. We are not examining in French.

TRESHAM   I think we shall be. But still!

CHAMBERS   I wish you would tell us what some of the ten made of suicide. I am a member of a Clerical and Medical Society, and we were discussing euthanasia last week. It is a very interesting and important subject.

RICHARDS   I second that. It concerns us doctors very intimately.

TRESHAM   Very well. I will read you two of the best, or parts of them. I was going to play golf, but it is much too wet.

MASTER   In that case we will adjourn to my study and smoke. I should like to hear the essays too.

TRESHAM   The first is so suspiciously well informed that I think he must have mugged up the subject with the help of Lecky, Westermarck, and Hastings. But it is rather well put together.

Skinner's Essay

There is perhaps no question of right or wrong on which more diametrically opposite opinions have been held than as to a man's right to declare his innings closed, as they say at cricket. The extremes are represented by the judge who tried the murderess Madame de Brinvilliers, and those who extolled the "noble death" of Cato. The judge in passing sentence said that the prisoner had done worse than murder her nearest relations; she had tried to murder herself.

In ancient Greece and Rome divergent views were held. Pythagoras is said to have forbidden men to desert the station in which God, their commander, placed them. Plato, without condemning suicide absolutely, held that it is justified only in extreme cases.

Aristotle holds that "a certain infamy attaches to the suicide, as one who acts unjustly towards the community". But Greek legend, and history too, teems with suicides. Among the later philosophers, the hedonists naturally taught that if life ceases to bring happiness it is sensible to put an end to it. The Cyrenaic Hegesias at Alexandria created such an epidemic of suicides by his lectures that the king of Egypt removed him from his post. Under the Empire the Stoics, among whom Seneca is conspicuous, congratulated themselves that no one need be miserable, since the way of escape is always open. Rome under the Cæsars was a nightmare to the upper classes. No life was safe; and a large number anticipated the doom which hung over their heads by a voluntary and sometimes theatrical death. Ovid, however, in an easily remembered couplet, says—

"Rebus in adversis facile est contemnere vitam;
    Fortiter ille facit qui miser esse potest."

Epictetus, while blaming those who take their own lives through cowardice, asserts vigorously the right of every man to decide for himself whether he shall go on living or not. Epicurus says that we should weigh carefully whether it is better to go to meet death or to wait for death to come to us. Plotinus is less uncompromising in his condemnation of suicide than Macrobius makes out; but he is clear that to depart from this life in a state of mental perturbation is unworthy of a philosopher.

Cases of theatrical suicide, almost as self-advertisement, are recorded. The best-known case is that of Peregrinus; but St. Paul's words about "giving my body to be burned" are believed by some commentators to refer to this strange practice.

Antiquity records many instances of suicide as an act of loyalty—of wives refusing to survive their husbands, of followers accompanying their chief to the grave, and the like. The world was startled when in 1912 the successful Japanese general Nogi and his wife committed *hara-kiri,* or *seppuku,* on the death of the emperor. The sacrifice of Hindu widows (*sati*) was sometimes voluntary, sometimes not.

Several women in antiquity are recorded to have committed suicide to preserve their chastity.

On the whole, the prevailing opinion in classical times was that it is a matter for the individual to decide for himself. Circumstances may arise which make life intolerable or dishonourable or a nuisance to others. In such cases suicide cannot be blamed and may be commended. But if troubles can be borne they should be borne.

Suicide is not forbidden in the Old Testament, though it is, with great severity, in the Koran. It seems to have been uncommon among the Hebrews. Ahithophel destroyed himself, and we are told that he was buried in the sepulchre of his fathers. There is no hint that the suicide of Judas enhanced the guilt of his treachery, though some Christian writers thought that it did. But from the first the Church held that the act was unlawful. Certain exceptions, however, were made. Those who rushed upon martyrdom which they might have escaped were not counted as suicides. Women who killed themselves to escape violation were not blamed until Augustine wrote that violence of this kind does not sully the soul and therefore should not be avoided in this desperate manner. All through the

Dark Ages, and indeed much later, a superstitious horror was attached to the crime, as it was now said to be. It was not till the reign of George IV that the law by which the suicide was to be buried at a cross-road with a stake through the body was repealed. The object was obviously to prevent the ghost of the departed from walking.

In the eighteenth century, with the growth of rationalism, there was a sharp reaction, and a tendency to revert to the ancient attitude towards suicide. Montesquieu and Voltaire justified the practice, and Hume wrote a well-known essay on the same side, in which he rebuts the religious arguments against it. In our own day opinion is divided; but whereas fifty years ago a case of suicide was considered to bring some discredit not only on the deceased but on his family, a more lenient judgment is now common. The number of suicides in proportion to the population is increasing, steadily but not rapidly, in most civilised nations. The notion, popularised by many French writers, that suicide is specially common in England is disproved by statistics. Some French authors would have their countrymen believe that in spite of the efforts of the police corpses of suicides are continually being taken out of the Thames. The lowest suicide rates are, I think, in countries where the people live under simple conditions such as cultivation of the soil by peasants, and where the authority of the priests is still strong enough to act as a deterrent. In countries where it is usual for men to carry lethal weapons the opportunities for suicide are increased, and a relatively high rate prevails. But it was observed during the Great War that in all the belligerent countries the suicide rate declined, an unexpected phenomenon which has not been explained. The increased use of gas ovens has provided an easy and painless death for those who are weary of life, and this is now the commonest method. But experience shows that suicides often take advantage of the easiest way without much consideration for its painlessness. Lysol is often used because it can be readily procured, though it means a painful death. There are fashions here as in other cases. Women hardly ever use firearms, and prefer drowning.

There is one curious ethical distinction for which it is not easy to account. Voluntary starvation, though a very deliberate method of suicide, is sometimes regarded as different from other modes of self-destruction. The Albigenses sometimes practised it under the name of Endura. Some of the militant suffragettes seem to have thought that by refusing to take food they might make the prison authorities responsible for their deaths. It would be interesting to know whether the Irish mayor who persisted in this course till he died received absolution from the Roman Church, though he obviously died in the practice of mortal sin. I think he did.

To sum up the ethical problem. The objection that a soldier must not leave the ranks without permission does not carry us far. A man may think that by continuing to live he is a burden rather than an asset to the community. An extreme instance is the voluntary self-sacrifice of Captain Oates on the return from the South Pole. In a sense his action was undoubtedly suicidal; but it was universally approved. It certainly cannot be said that a sense of public duty would in all cases make suicide impossible. Hume suggests that if it is an interference with Providence to shorten our lives, it is equally so when we use medical science to prolong them. This, however, is by no means obvious. He thinks that the horror of suicide is mainly superstitious. No doubt superstition has had much to do with it; but we have to consider the cause of the superstition. On the whole we may expect that public opinion will more and more approximate to the point of view current in antiquity.

TRESHAM I have read to you the greater part of Skinner's essay, because it contains more facts than any of the others. But the ethical question is not adequately treated. For instance, why was there such a superstitious horror of suicide in the Dark and Middle Ages, and why has this feeling almost disappeared from modern societies? What do you say about that, Mr. Chambers?

CHAMBERS I have given up trying to understand the mentality of the Middle Ages; it is more incomprehensible than that of the modern Russians, as illustrated by their novels. People in Russia seem to act from motives quite different from those which operate in western Europe and America. But the Middle Ages are far more bizarre. There was a violence and exaggeration about every aspect of their life. Horrible cruelty and mawkish sentimentalism went hand in hand. Huizinga describes how "at Brussels a young incendiary and murderer was placed in the centre of a circle of burning faggots and straw, and made fast to a stake by a chain running round an iron ring. He addressed touching words to the spectators, and so softened their hearts that everyone burst into tears, and his death was commended as the finest that was ever seen". We learn from the recently discovered manuscript of Margery Kempe how "boisterous" weeping and groaning were considered appropriate on many occasions. Revenge was a sacred duty; feudal

fidelity the chief virtue. Torture and executions were
enjoyed as a popular entertainment. Confession and
extreme unction, both in France and England, were
refused to a criminal condemned to death. When a
gang of brigands was executed in France "the people
laughed a good deal because they were all poor men".
A locksmith of Blois "furnished two collars, one to
make fast Belon the fool, the other to put round the
neck of the monkey of her Grace the Duchess". There
was in the Middle Ages a peculiar horror of death;
and as for outrages upon the corpses of malefactors,
that was common form until the eighteenth century.
But as for the attitude towards suicide, I think the
strongest feeling was that for a man deliberately to die
in mortal sin, in circumstances which forbid the
possibility of repentance and absolution, is the most
complete act of apostasy which can be imagined. The
notion that our eternal destiny depends not on our
lives as a whole but on the state of mind in which we
leave the world accounts for a great deal. The peni-
tent thief, whose repentance in the hour of death
procured his admission to Paradise, was often
referred to.

RICHARDS I demur to Skinner's suggestion that
Catholicism acts as a powerful deterrent to suicide.
There is probably some little truth in it; there is very
little suicide in Ireland, and still less in Spain. But the
rate is also very low in Protestant Northern Ireland,
and in Protestant Norway; whereas in Sweden, another
Lutheran country, the number of suicides is very high.
The rate is low in Protestant England and in pre-
dominantly Protestant Holland, high in Catholic
France and Protestant Germany, especially in Saxony.
These very sharp differences in adjacent countries have

never been fully explained; religion does not seem to have much to do with them. I think we must look to medical psychology to throw some light on the problem. Although the majority of suicides are certainly not insane, they are probably not quite normal; and there seems to be a real contagiousness in the state of mind which leads to self-destruction. Where suicide is considered a natural escape from trouble it will be more frequently resorted to. I know of no other way of accounting for the great difference in the statistics for Sweden and for Norway. Otherwise, the low figures in North-Western Europe may be regarded as a part of the distinctive civilisation of those countries, which form a group apart.

TRESHAM I think you may like to hear part of another essay, which handles the question from a different side. It discusses the ethical problem of euthanasia, which is obviously included in the scope of the subject.

Crosse's Essay

Suicide is a way of dying. Sometimes it is the normal termination of a psychosis which makes the patient so miserable that he cannot endure to live. In these cases the verdict of temporary insanity is correct, and no moral judgment is in place. Our juries often bring in a verdict of suicide while temporarily insane in order to remove any stigma from the memory of the deceased or to soothe the feelings of his family. Until within living memory there was another motive: the property of the *felo de se* was confiscated by the State. England lags behind most other nations in reforming its criminal law; reforms which affect no one's pocket arouse no interest. Attempted suicide is a crime in England and in hardly any other civilised country. In cases where the suicide is quite sane, moral censure may be imposed or withheld. A few persons kill themselves every year from disappointed love—an aberration of romanticism. Financiers are rather prone to choose this escape when they are, or think they are, bankrupt. The death of a dearly loved relative, especially of a husband or wife, convinces some that life is no longer worth living. Remorse induces some to execute upon themselves the sentence which they feel that they deserve. Many have ended their lives to escape from what they conceived as dishonour, and this motive has often been regarded as not only reasonable but honourable. In Japan a person who has been insulted will sometimes choose this strange method of avenging an injury. Many murderers kill themselves to escape from arrest; many more—and other criminals too—would do so if they were not prevented, either before their trial or after receiving their sentence. The question may fairly be raised whether a criminal ought to be prevented from executing sentence upon himself. It seems to me barbarous and unfeeling cruelty. If a man has already been condemned to death, it is hardly suicide for him to anticipate the hangman, and whatever we may think of capital punishment, its object is not to inflict the extremity of humiliation on the culprit or his family. It may be objected that if this liberty were granted it would increase the number of homicides. But in this country the number of executions is so small that this argument has very little force. In the case of criminals who are condemned to imprisonment, it is said that many would prefer death. If this is so, the punishment of imprisonment is unjustly severe, since the intention is to inflict a penalty less extreme than death. This is just a case where unintentional cruelty is acquiesced in because it is no one's interest to have it remedied. I do not say that a criminal is morally justified in wishing to die rather than serve his sentence; but it is not the province of the prison authorities to prevent him. I should certainly have allowed the criminous suffragettes to starve themselves in prison if they wished to do so; to liberate them was merely absurd.

But I wish in this short essay to confine myself to one aspect of the question on which public opinion is at present sharply divided. When a man or woman is dying slowly and in great suffering from an incurable disease, is it the duty of the patient to wait till death at last comes to his or her relief, and is it the duty of the medical attendant to prolong life by every means in his power till the last moment? There have been three or four cases lately when a man or woman has been tried for the murder of a near relative whose sufferings were unbearable to watch. Most doctors in large practice have probably been entreated by patients to shorten their agonies, and they must have wished sometimes that they were allowed to do so. But as the law stands, the owner of a horse or dog who does not put the animal out of its misery may be fined for cruelty, and if he shows this mercy to a human being imploring to be released he may be hanged for murder. It is, I believe, not uncommon for doctors to give an overdose of morphine to a suffering cancer patient, though they must do so at their own risk. I have heard that some horribly mutilated soldiers in the Great War were given the "happy dispatch". In the German army this was certainly done. Monstrous births are quietly nipped in the bud by the accoucheur, and if an infant's head is too large to permit it to come into the world in the normal way an instrument called a cranioclast may be employed. The Roman Church, it is true, orders that if the life either of the mother or of the infant must be sacrificed the infant must be preferred; but one cannot imagine modern medical practice acting on this principle.

It seems to follow that the sanctity of human life is not an absolute principle to which no exceptions can be admitted. If so, the question of euthanasia may be debated on utilitarian grounds, and the conclusion can hardly be avoided that in some circumstances it is not only permissible but demanded for reasons of humanity. When life is a torment, and every useful occupation is impossible, why condemn the sufferer to drink the cup of pain to the dregs?

Nevertheless, I do not think that Christian ethics will ever sanction the practice. Is suffering an evil? The ancients, with few exceptions, said Yes, of course. But we must not forget Plato's words that except through suffering there is no remedy for moral evil. But Christianity finds in suffering an elevating and liberating influence, as the setting free of a deeply inward and mysterious power. The incapacity to suffer, the impossibility of bearing pain, grief, and misfortune, is plainly a weakness of the character. But the man who can bear suffering is strengthened by it. Even when there is nothing left to the sufferer except to suffer bravely, a deeper level in his moral nature is released; a new kind of strength is revealed. Deep places are opened, in his own heart and in the hearts of others. "Without suffering," says a German proverb, "no one is ennobled." We meet sometimes people who have just missed nobility of character because life has been made too easy and pleasant for them. There remains another argument, which was drawn out long ago in a once famous little book, James Hinton's *Mystery of Pain*, based on the verse in St. Paul about "filling up that which was lacking in the afflictions of Christ for his body's sake". The author, himself a great sufferer, comforted himself by thinking that all suffering patiently borne has a kind of redemptive value, and contributes something to the price which humanity must pay for its redemption and progress. This is an argument which will have no meaning for many people, but I think a Christian ought to understand it and treat it with respect.

RICHARDS I should certainly wish to treat it with respect. But does it go far enough? If suffering has a positive value, is it not wrong to use anæsthetics? Ought we to inject morphine into our cancer patients? We remember that in the last century many women refused anæsthetics when they were in labour; they thought they ought not to evade the curse of Eve. It was said that Queen Victoria had this scruple. But nobody now, I imagine, would agree that it is morally wrong to take advantage of anæsthetics.

MASTER Rightly or wrongly, there has been a great change as to the moral value of suffering. Dr. Pusey, I believe, flogged himself in his college rooms, but I should think he was almost the last to do so in the Anglican Church. I do not know whether the "discipline" is still much used in Catholic monasteries. The last remnant of Protestant asceticism disappeared when hot-water taps were introduced into our baths, and the English gentleman no longer broke the ice in his tub.

RICHARDS I should like to ask your brother

whether he could bring himself to talk about the strengthening and ennobling effect of suffering to a sick man who was dying of cancer of the tongue, or gangrene?

CHAMBERS   I could, and I have. But I cannot say that I felt happy about it, or confident that if I were in the same state I could hear such talk without impatience.

RICHARDS   I am glad you confess so much. The majority of death-beds are not distressing to the on-looker. Very many people die in a state of coma, or just drop off quietly. But now and then the last hours, and even days, are very cruel, and one longs to see the sufferer released. I have myself given a large dose of morphine, with the result which I expected. You told us, Mr. Chambers, that you have been discussing the subject at a society of clergymen and doctors. What conclusion did you come to?

CHAMBERS   We came to no conclusion. I expected to find that all the doctors were in favour of euthanasia and all the parsons against it. But it was not so at all. Two of the parsons said that whatever view we might take about the spiritual value of suffering, useless and avoidable torture cannot be the will of God. One parson had spent an hour in the museum of the College of Surgeons, to help him to make up his mind. He came out horrified, and convinced that in some cases, unusual cases perhaps, it was senseless and cruel to prolong life. On the other hand, our doctors were far from unanimous in favour of euthanasia. One of them said we can never be absolutely sure that the con-dition of a patient is hopeless. The others shook their heads at this.

RICHARDS   No wonder. That remark was hardly ingenuous.

CHAMBERS   Another had never heard of opiates being given to send a sufferer into a sleep from which he would not awake. Two others seemed bothered by the oath of Hippocrates. The physician must always try to prolong life, never in any circumstances shorten it. Then the discussion took a turn with which ethics has not much to do. If euthanasia were legalised, the patient and his nearest relative would have to sign a request for it. But the nearest relative might have sinister reasons for wishing to get the sick person out of the way; there might be a legacy waiting for him. And the patient might be induced to sign the paper without knowing what he was doing. Besides, melancholia is not always incurable; the patient might wish to die because he was temporarily miserable, and not for any adequate reason.

RICHARDS   Such mistakes as that could be guarded against.

MASTER   I remember a sentence in Paulsen's discussion of the subject. "Heldenthum ist nicht Pflicht". It may be heroic for a man in great bodily agony to bear it to the last, but we cannot say that it is a duty. I don't know what I should do myself; but I think that would be my attitude if a friend were in that state. If he decided to go, I could not take it upon myself to blame him. As for altering the law so as to make euthanasia possible, I should be in favour of it, though I quite see that safeguards are necessary.

TRESHAM   Well, I don't think I need trouble you with any more of the essays. It was perhaps not a very happily chosen subject. I should not wonder if we were to elect the Balliol philosopher to whom "French of Paris is unknown".

JOHN, JONATHAN,
AND FRITZ

SPEAKERS: *John Smith and James Brown, Englishmen;
Wilbur K. Merrill, an American; Hans Müller, a German
refugee.*

SMITH   When the history of our times comes to be
written, these wars will be called civil wars, the co-
operative suicide of the white peoples. The war with
Japan belongs to another chapter.

BROWN   What an appalling exacerbation of hatred
we see everywhere. There was nothing at all like it in
the Napoleonic wars.

SMITH   Total war is a very different thing from the
old wars, fought by professional armies. It is one thing
to look on at a rough game of football, and quite
another to have your home burnt and your family
murdered in their beds.

BROWN   When the nations realise that war is not
a game, but the most horrible kind of mass murder,
perhaps they will at last decide that they have had
enough of it.

SMITH   I hope so. But that is not quite what I was
driving at. In the last century it was hoped that
national animosities were dying out. They were plainly
irrational. On the one side, trade and commerce and
banking were international. Frontiers and tariffs were
merely a nuisance. We hoped that other nations would
see the advantages of free trade. And on the other side

there was the slogan, "Workers of the world, unite". Was not the war of classes much more reasonable than the wars of nations ? Was there not much more community of interest between the English and the German wage-earner than between either of them and the English manufacturer and the German Junker? Did not many people think that big business and international Socialism would for once agree that war is absurd and ruinous? Hitler and Mussolini knew better; they knew that national hatred is stronger than self-interest and stronger than class loyalty. But is it not a queer thing? We might parody a verse in the New Testament and say, "He that hateth not his neighbour whom he hath seen, why should he hate the foreigner whom he hath not seen?" If he does meet the foreigner, he does not hate him at all.

BROWN It has gone so far that all alliances are unstable. There was never much love lost between us and the French, and now the dominant section in France is actively hostile to its late allies. The Italians hate the Germans far more than they hate us; and the Hungarians and Rumanians, who are both fighting for Germany, loathe each other.

MERRILL How about the alliance between my country and yours? Is that likely to be stable and permanent?

SMITH It is probably not absolutely necessary for you, though you have made up your minds that while Germany and Japan are in their present moods isolationism is hardly a practical policy. The downfall of Great Britain would not only extinguish liberty in the old world; it would be very inconvenient for you. Neither the "herring-pond" nor the Pacific is broad enough in these days. But for us the maintenance of the alliance is essential, unless we are content to be an island on the outskirts of Europe. I doubt if it is generally realised that we can never go to war again without the concurrence of the United States and of our own Dominions, and that this consent is not likely to be given to any active interference in continental politics. Our Dominions refused to help us in a war to save the Czechs. It is quite possible that they may some day prefer an alliance with America. This is obviously true of Canada, and it now seems that we cannot protect our Australasian Dominions without American help.

BROWN At the back of our minds, Merrill, is the dream of a Commonwealth of the English-speaking nations. America would be the predominant partner, but this island would always be the mother country, the object, I hope, of loyalty and affection. This dream comes naturally to us, because we have never looked upon the United States as a foreign country. But I am afraid we are foreigners to you.

MERRILL Yes, you don't realise what a *colluvies gentium*, what a hotch-potch our country is. What you say is true. When an Englishman settles in America he does not feel that he has lost his nationality. He becomes a hundred per cent American because he remains a hundred per cent Briton. But the German remains always a hyphenated American, and so does the Italian. As for the Irish, you know what they count for in our politics.

SMITH Yes, indeed. I have been reading the Letters of Spring Rice, who, as you remember, was our Ambassador at Washington. He was an Irishman himself, but he says, "Nothing we could do would conciliate the Irish; they have blood in their eyes when they look our way. An Irishman would refuse to go to heaven if St. Peter were an Englishman". In the United States "there is an Irish vote, but no English vote". The reason for that you gave yourself just now.

MERRILL You don't think they have any excuse?

SMITH No, I don't. We have treated them with unparalleled patience ever since I can remember. Is it not rather absurd to bring up Oliver Cromwell against us now?

MERRILL It is; but your memories are rather conveniently short.

SMITH I want to quote something else from Spring Rice. It is unpleasant, but I want you to understand us. "The native American is always ready to hear an attack upon England. This country is afraid of Germany, but the impression prevails that Great Britain would never resent any injury from the United States, and therefore any injury could safely be done her. Congress will be hostile, because they believe that hostility to England entails no danger. They will be friendly to Germans, because they know that German resentment will entail serious consequences."

MERRILL That is certainly unpleasant, and he could hardly have written like that after 1917. We have decided to face the "serious consequences". I don't think Spring Rice was an unqualified success at Washington. He was a fine type of English gentleman, honourable, high-minded, and patriotic; but he was naturally pessimistic, and his health was giving way. He found foreign politics a disgusting business. Like most of your countrymen he believed that, in his own words, "the English line is a sort of stolid honesty, a little bit inclined to be stupid. When we try to be clever it doesn't come off; it is like a dog standing on its hind legs".

MÜLLER   Well, well, that is not what we think of you, nor what any other nation thinks of you. You are the cleverest humbugs in creation.

SMITH   You shall have your say presently, Müller. I believe Spring Rice was perfectly right. Here are a few more of his remarks, written not from Washington but from Stockholm between 1904 and 1909. "Russia and France act on the principle that it is safe to insult anyone who won't fight." "I wish people would learn defensive patriotism—to love their own mothers without hating other people's. The Germans are exactly the contrary; they have a perpetual well of malice springing in their hearts." "The sum of the whole tendency here is to organise a continental alliance against England." "Bismarck, impenetrable to the assaults of affection, allowed himself one luxury of emotion—to hate." Emil Ludwig, in his Life of Bismarck, says the same. "The sanction of treaties and written promises is force and nothing but force." "Here is all the world talking of war between England and Germany—except in England. And yet if we fall, the fall is final."

MERRILL   So we were not the only villains.

SMITH   We never thought you were. But you ought to be better than the others, and until lately your Government has behaved pretty badly to the old country. I have heard it said that the American likes England but dislikes the English; the Englishman likes Americans but dislikes America. We certainly like Americans, and we have our grievances against America.

MERRILL   Well, America, as you know, is a very

143

large country. I think it is true that till the end of the
last century you had something to complain of. The
school books were anti-British, and our politicians
found it good sport, and a short cut to popularity, to
twist the lion's tail. But now we must distinguish. If
you go to New England, or to any part of the Atlantic
coast, you will be received with gracious hospitality.
You will find the educated people well informed on
European affairs; you will find that they have read
the best English books; and above all you will feel
every day that you and they are sharers in a common
civilisation. They look at most things very much as
you do; you will be more at home among them than
in any European country except perhaps Scandinavia.
It is not a small thing that some of the best living
writers of pure English—Thornton Wilder and Walter
Lippmann are the first names that occur to me—are
Americans. I can't say much about the South, as I
never lived there. But I think if the visiting Englishman
has the sense to keep his mouth shut about the negroes
he will be made welcome. There are of course a few
families descended from the planters of slave-owning
days whose manners and outlook are those of rather
old-fashioned aristocrats. If you go to the Pacific Slope
you will find a different state of things. The dwellers
in that earthly Paradise turn uneasy eyes towards the
western ocean. On the other side live people who if
they were admitted would make life impossible for the
white man. If before the war you had asked a Cali-
fornian what he would do if the Japanese invaded
Australia he would have said, "We should certainly
not let Australia go, and I think the whole country
would be behind us". It is only in the Middle West,
that large and increasingly important part of the

United States, that you might find unfriendly feeling and possibly rudeness. The people there are very much wrapped up in their own affairs; they think very little about Europe; and the newspapers which they read are not pleasant reading for an Englishman. But on the whole I believe that the alliance, not so much with England as with the British Commonwealth, will continue and grow firmer. Half our people are not Anglo-Saxons; the purest Anglo-Saxons in America, by the way, may be the Fundamentalist farmers of Kentucky and Tennessee, whom you are so fond of laughing at; but the English-speaking nations will be drawn together by the knowledge that their civilisation, with all that they care for, is threatened. The majority of the non-British citizens of the United States are as much devoted to liberty and democracy as the descendants of the old colonists. We have really succeeded in making a nation out of immigrants from all parts of Europe.

SMITH   We are very glad to hear you say that about the future. It is what we all hope.

MERRILL   But now about another thing that you said—that the Americans don't like the English whom they know. It is true that the manners of the English often put us off. Keyserling observed it and he says: "The English and the Americans speak the same language, but are entirely different in all other respects, such as the lack of reserve among Americans and the extreme cultivation of it by Englishmen; extreme privacy in England, extreme publicity in America; the highly developed political sense of the Englishman, and the absolute want of it in the American; the lack of any essential likeness between the two peoples."

BROWN   A great exaggeration, I should say. Key-serling is judging from a small class of Englishmen. The average Englishman is not at all reserved, and is very gregarious. The differences are superficial, not essential.

MERRILL   Still, your people do often give the impression of being haughty and distant. We suspect them of despising all other nations, and of being convinced that they are the salt of the earth. "Blessed are the meek, for they shall inherit the earth. That means us." "If God has a hard job on hand, He gives it to His Englishmen." Milton, I believe.

BROWN   Most unfair! We are not arrogant at all. We don't despise other nations. It is true that you like "good mixers" and we don't. Many of us would like to have reserved railway carriages for "talkers". But when we know and like a man you don't find us stiff, do you?

MERRILL   No, indeed, but you do put us off at first.

BROWN   We are wrong, I admit, but we are made that way.

SMITH   Brown, we are whipped for the sins of our grandfathers. The Victorian Englishman, until the Boer War knocked the stuffing out of him, was a rather intolerable person. Look at the cartoons in *Punch* at the time of the American Civil War, and later too. Remember how Palmerston used cheerfully to insult and lecture all the Powers of Europe. Yes, and later, what rubbish we talked about the white man's burden, and with what smug complacency we set to work to paint the map of the world red. In the last twenty years of Victoria's reign we had a ridiculous attack of aggressive imperialism. The popular songs at the beginning of the Boer War really touched bottom for vulgarity and effrontery. However, we are not like that at all now.

BROWN It sounds an absurd thing to say about the greatest nation in the world, but really many Americans suffer from a kind of inferiority complex. It is this that makes some of them talk boastfully. We look upon our country much as we look upon our wives. We are privately convinced that our wife is the best woman in the world, but we don't say so to the world, and we are quite content that other men should have the same opinion about their wives. Indeed, if Müller will forgive me, we wish that some of the anti-Hitler German writers were not quite so savage against their own country. I will give you an instance of American misplaced humility. I was walking in the Cotswolds with a young American professor, who has since died. We were passing through a village with a famous parish church. The rector met us in the street, and said civilly, "I believe you gentlemen are Americans. May I have the pleasure of showing you my beautiful church?" My friend was quite disturbed; he thought I should dislike being taken for an American! The Canadians have the same reputation. A friend who visited Canada complained that they took offence where none was intended. "I thought it wisest," he said, "to expunge the words Canada and England from my vocabulary; but they don't like that either."

MERRILL The truth is that we generalise far too readily. National character is mainly an illusion. In the Great War Clemenceau found all his ideas upset. "The Englishman was noted for his calm, but English soldiers tended to be hysterical more than any others. The Americans were supposed to be so quick and they were so slow. The French were supposed to be gay and they were solemn." It is true that there is an unfortunate tradition about English pride, and I agree that it should now be forgotten.

BROWN Smith and I are encouraged by your sympathy to the idea of a permanent alliance. It seems to us to be the one hope for humanity. Standing alone we cannot remain a Great Power. Our home base is too small. The conditions which gave us a great advantage over continental nations no longer exist, and the discovery of flying is a misfortune to us. When Blériot flew over the Channel a few wise men shook their heads. But just think of the prospect if all the English-speaking nations stand together. A real League of Nations in being. Over two hundred million people —I don't count the Indians—united to maintain peace, liberty, toleration, and decent behaviour in a tormented world. I believe we could do it. I believe we could abolish war. Economic sanctions could be applied on a very large scale if necessary. Lincoln's famous words about government of the people, by the people, for the people appeal to all who speak our tongue, the tongue, as Wordsworth reminds us, that Shakespeare spoke, and who cherish the faith and morals that Milton held. Those great names belong to America as well as to England. I have marked a passage from a speech by General Smuts in 1917. "All the empires we have known in the past and that exist to-day are founded on the idea of assimilation. Your whole idea and basis are entirely different. You do not want to standardise the nations of the British Empire; you want to develop them towards greater, fuller nationhood. These communities, the offspring of the mother country, or territories like my own, which have been annexed after the vicissitudes of war, must not be moulded on any one pattern. You want them to develop freely on the principles of self-government, and therefore your whole idea is different from anything that has existed before. That is the fundamental fact we have to bear in mind—that this British Commonwealth of Nations does not stand for standardisation or denationalisation, but for the fuller, richer and more various life of all the nations comprised in it. Even the nations which have fought against it, like my own, must feel that their cultural interests, their language, their religion, are as safe and as secure under the British flag as those of the children of your own household and your own blood. Therefore it seems to me that there is only one solution, and that is a solution supplied by your past traditions—the traditions of freedom, self-government, and of the fullest development of all constituent parts of the Empire."* A noble passage, which shows how wise we were to trust the Dutch, that tough, indomitable nation whose fleet gave us so much trouble in the seventeenth century. But I ask you, Merrill, is not this a League of Nations which your great Republic ought to join? You remind us that you are no longer Anglo-Saxons. But how far is the British Commonwealth Anglo-Saxon? South Africa is predominantly Dutch. There is only one country in which the French are increasing rapidly— that is Canada, under our flag. We have doubled the population of India, Palestine and Egypt. Even the Maoris of New Zealand are now increasing rapidly. It is even possible, I think, that our League of Nations, with the United States at its head, might draw in other

* From *The Pattern of Freedom*, chosen by Bruce L. Richmond (Faber and Faber).

149

nations which have much the same ideals. There is
Latin America, parts of which are becoming a melting-
pot of nationalities. There is the north-western European
group, Scandinavia and possibly Holland and Belgium.
These small nations all love liberty and hate war. May
it not be the God-appointed destiny of the nations
founded by Britain to bring to an end the era of
aggressive nationalism and to establish at last the
promise of the angels' song, "Peace on earth and good-
will to men"? Think of the alternative, the total
destruction of freedom, humanity and religion in
Europe; the domination of the continent by the most
brutal, cruel, and searching tyranny that the world
has ever seen. Would these enemies of the human race
feel secure while the institutions and loyalties which
they have destroyed in Europe exist anywhere—even
three thousand miles from Europe? Believe me, the
fall of the British Commonwealth would be an irre-
parable disaster for the whole world. As your famous
writer Santayana says: "The Englishman is no
missionary, no conqueror. He is rather glad if natives
will remain natives and strangers strangers; yet out-
wardly he is most hospitable and accepts almost
everybody for the time being. He carries his English
weather in his heart wherever he goes, and it becomes
a cool spot in the desert, and a steady and sane oracle
among all the deliriums of mankind. Never since the
heroic days of Greece has the world had such a sweet,
just, boyish master. It will be a black day for the
human race when scientific blackguards, conspirators,
churls, and fanatics manage to supplant him."* Forgive me, Merrill, if I have been too patriotic. I have
picked out a Dutchman and an American to sing the

* Santayana, *Soliloquies in England*, page 32.

praises which privately I think we deserve, but which we could hardly proclaim for ourselves.

MÜLLER   You told me that you would let me speak when you had done. You know what my career has been. I worked with the Nazis for some time, because I thought they had lifted the German people out of the slough of despond, put an end to unemployment and class warfare, and enabled us to take our proper place as one of the leading nations of the world. By degrees I discovered that we had fallen into the hands of a corrupt and ruthless gang, who were making the name of my beloved country stink in the nostrils of all decent people. I gave up everything, my home, my property, and my friends, in order to escape from a land where I could hardly call my soul my own. I shall have some things to say which you may not like, but I think you will admit that I have a right to say them.

The Englishman is normally a good-natured and amicable fellow. Until lately he has believed that the horrors of war were things which foreigners (whom you can never really trust) do to each other, but which Britons neither do nor suffer. You see you have never been invaded since William the Conqueror, and your last civil war, a mild and gentlemanly affair, was in the seventeenth century. You also have a higher standard of living than any other European country—about 30 per cent higher than Germany and France, and three times the figure for Italy. That, it seems to you, is a very proper distribution of the good things of the world; no right-thinking person would wish to disturb it. So you are pacifists, and I know there is a strong vein of genuine idealism mixed with self-regarding motives.

But do you realise that when the Englishman is

thoroughly roused he is a very ugly customer ? The Indians who remember the Mutiny do not think that he is a very gentle ruler. In the Great War you were furious about the submarine campaign, but did you realise (I don't think you did) that hundreds of thousands of our non-combatants died from malnutrition in consequence of your blockade ? When the armistice was signed, Churchill and Lloyd George were in favour of sending food ships at once to Germany; but such was the hatred of Germany in England that they dared not do it. It was the worst blunder you made in the war. Germans in England during the war were worse treated than the English in Germany. I know you thought they were all spies; most of them were not. I hope you are all ashamed of the hysterical screams of 1919: "Hang the Kaiser", "Make Germany pay", "Squeeze them till the pips squeak", and so on. There is something vulgar and extravagant about British mass-psychology, quite contrary to the usual opinion about the character of your nation. Either you have changed, or a submerged stratum has now come to the surface and become vocal.

But I want especially to protest against the opinion, now very widely held, that the German, or, as they say, the Prussianised German, is incorrigibly brutal and aggressive; that he has always been like that and always will be. Such a delusion is very unscientific and unjust; it may seriously interfere with the conclusion of a reasonable peace. You do not know enough about Germany under the Weimar republic. I have not got with me the report which the Indian poet Rabindranath Tagore wrote after his visit to Germany in 1921. The gist of it was that the Germans seemed to have abandoned their militarist ambitions and their materialistic outlook; they were, he thought, now hoping for a spiritual and intellectual revival, a return to the pre-Bismarckian Germany. About the same time Adolf Hitler in *Mein Kampf* said impatiently that when the last German disappeared the last pacifist would go too. Or consider the book about England by Dibelius, the brilliant professor of English literature at Berlin, the first edition of which appeared in the same year. Although the Allies won the war and Germany lost it, I doubt whether any English publisher in 1921 would have accepted so fair and favourable an account of Germany as this about England. The English nation, he says, is "one of the sanest of nations, a healthy people. Throughout the British Isles there prevails a robust, masculine, and sound morality. It is no mean achievement to have made self-control the instinct of a whole nation, which only rarely yields to volcanic outbursts of primitive strength." "It is a type of character on the whole the highest yet attained." We have no sectional code of ethics, one for the soldier, one for the merchant, one for the scholar; we have only one standard, that of the gentleman. He ends his book by saying, "It would be a loss to the world if there were no powerful England, but it would be a lasting detriment to the world if England were to become all-powerful".

SMITH Excuse me, Müller, but what nonsense the last sentence is. Who ever dreams of England becoming all-powerful? I can't understand you Germans. At one time you speak as if we were an ambitious Power, aiming at universal conquest; at another time, as Rauschning shows, we are to be an insignificant island, inhabited by a few million agriculturists.

MÜLLER We do sometimes talk nonsense about politics. The average German is non-political; he regards politics as a rather dirty business which does not concern him. But my point in quoting Dibelius was to show that Germans after the war took a generous and fair view of their former enemies, while your countrymen were still foaming at the mouth.

SMITH That was in 1921. How came they to change so completely?

MÜLLER Remember the humiliations that the French put upon us. Remember the ridiculous demands for wildly impossible indemnities; the invasion of the Ruhr; the brothels for black troops forced upon German homes. Remember the agony of 1923, when money lost all its value, and the most industrious and respectable classes were reduced to beggary. Then, after a false dawn of prosperity, encouraged by foolish foreign loans, came the return of misery in 1929. It was not a normal Germany that put Hitler in power; it is not a normal Germany that submits to and seems to support him. No one can feel more strongly than I do the disgrace that has befallen my country; but when you speak of an English-speaking alliance as the only chance for civilisation in the future against the destructive barbarism of the "Huns" I am sure you are making a mistake. After all, there is perhaps no nation to which civilisation—what we call culture— owes more than to Germany. Are we really rotten through and through? Do you think so after meeting us socially, after visiting our country, after reading our books? The danger to civilisation, in my opinion, comes not from fits of aggressive imperialism, which at one time you thought the inherent vice of the French, who are now the most pacific people in Europe. It comes from irrational hatred between nations. Goethe said that these hatreds were strongest among barbarians. May I express a hope that you will not set the example of inextinguishable hatred against Germany? The large majority of Germans do not love war. They want to live quietly and peaceably in their homes, like all other nations that I know of. They are not gloating over the enslavement of other peoples. Their victories in this war, from all I have heard, leave them cold.

BROWN Thank you, Müller. You have told us some home truths, but faithful are the wounds of a friend. I don't think we are really vindictive; we have short memories, as Merrill told us. And my English-speaking League would threaten nobody. We want no unwilling subjects. I shall not forget your appeal to bury the hatchet after the war, but I am afraid it will be difficult; you have seen London.

CRADLES AND
COFFINS

I

This and the following Talk perhaps need some justification. I was a friend of Sir Francis Galton, the founder of Eugenics; we were near neighbours in Rutland Gate when I was incumbent of a West End parish. Until lately I have been on the Council of the Eugenics Society. In 1913 the National Council of Public Morals instituted a "National Birth Rate Commission, for the promotion of Race Regeneration, Spiritual, Moral, and Physical". I was chairman of this Commission, which included some very well-known names, and the meetings were held at my house. We heard a great deal of evidence from medical men, statisticians, social workers, ministers of religion, and others. The Report was published in 1916 by Chapman and Hall, with the title *The Declining Birth Rate, its Causes and Effects*. My interest in the subject has been sustained during the twenty-five years which have passed since the publication of this Report.

I append a list of a few of the books which I have found useful, but the literature of the subject is enormous.

Proceedings of the World Population Conference at Geneva, 1927.

Problems of Population, being Report of the Second General Assembly of the International Union for the Scientific Investigation of Population Problems, 1931.

156

Congrès International de la Population, Paris, 1938. 8 volumes.

[The Congress at Berlin in 1935, under Nazi auspices, is said to have produced very little of scientific value.]

The Eugenics Review.

Population, 1933-1938.

Havelock Ellis, *The Task of Social Hygiene* and other Works.

C. B. Davenport, *Heredity in Relation to Eugenics, 1912.*

R. Pearl, *The Biology of Population Growth; The Natural History of Population, 1939.*

A. M. Carr Saunders, *The Population Problem, 1922; World Population, 1936.*

H. Cox, *The Problem of Population, 1923.*

Max Hirsch, *Präventiv-verkehr und Fruchtabtreibung.*

SPEAKERS: *A lecturer for the Eugenics Society, and a heckler.*

THE LECTURER Ladies and Gentlemen—I am here on behalf of the Eugenics Society, but of course the Society is in no way committed to my views. The accepted definition of Eugenics is "the study of agencies under social control that may improve or impair the qualities of future generations either physically or morally". Sir Francis Galton, who invented the name, is generally regarded as the founder of the science. He said that the influences which determine human qualities may be classified under the words "Nature" and "Nurture", and he thought that Nature is the more important of the two. In the opinion of many modern students he and his first disciples attributed to "Nature" much that more properly belongs to "Nurture", or environment, and therefore overestimated the importance of heredity. The son of a successful man has every inducement to follow in his father's footsteps, and is often helped by other scholars and men of science. The son of a Cabinet Minister has a good start in political life. On the other side, vicious and criminal stocks, like the notorious Jukeses, have probably never had a fair chance. The older generation of eugenists were accused of a tendency to identify "the economic élite with the psycho-physical élite", which they never intended to do.

In any case, new discoveries, especially those of Mendel, and of his successors who have studied those ultra-microscopic entities, chromosomes and genes, have made the subject more difficult and complicated than it seemed to be in Galton's day. Some men of science, notably Jennings in America, throw cold water on the attempts of eugenists to frame a practical policy. Others are becoming more environmental and political.

The study has several branches. Besides the broad division into "Nature" and "Nurture", there are positive and negative Eugenics. The aim of the former is to encourage desirable births, the aim of the latter to discourage undesirable births. This may be considered the main business and the chief interest of Eugenics. But though quality, not quantity, is the aim, such questions as the differential fertility of classes and nations obviously concern us. If superior races, or classes, or nations are in danger of dying out, the efforts of the eugenist must come to nothing. It is on this subject, the ominous decline in the birth-rate, that I am to speak to you to-day. I assume that my audience is intelligent, but that you have not made a special study of an intricate subject. I also assume that you want to know the truth, even if it is not very pleasant. I shall accordingly give you some facts which a specialist would think rather rudimentary.

I need not speak of the prodigious fertility of some of the lower animals. "If all the progeny of an oyster survived and multiplied," says Wallace, "its great-great-grandchildren would make a heap of shells eight times the size of the world." Every organic being, as Darwin says, naturally increases at so high a rate that if not destroyed the earth would soon be covered by the progeny of a single pair. Not very "soon" in the case of elephants and a few other slow-breeding animals, but within a measurable time.

In our own species what Malthus called checks have always operated. Periodical famines were formerly common in India and still occur in China. The latest examples in Europe were the Russian famine after the Bolshevik revolution, and those caused by the present war in Greece and other countries. Pestilence has periodically checked population all through history. There were great plagues in Europe in the second century and in the sixth. The Black Death in the fourteenth century may have destroyed one-third of the population. We have got rid of plague and cholera in Europe, and of typhus, except in war-time; but the epidemic which it was agreed to call influenza, which is not caused by a single kind of microbe, killed some fifteen million people in 1918, more than the deaths in the Great War. Whether the sweating sickness, so much dreaded in the Middle Ages, was influenza, no one seems to know.

The destructiveness of war can be estimated only if we include in the death-roll not only those killed in action and massacred but deaths of soldiers and sailors from sickness and the births prevented by the absence of husbands. The Russo-Japanese War was the first in which the deaths from disease did not exceed those caused by wounds. You will find Dumas and Vedel-Petersen's book very instructive on this subject. In the Boer War we lost rather over 6,000 killed in action and 14,000 from disease. The Boers lost at most 4,000 killed and, I regret to say, many thousands in the concentration camps. The Great War cost nearly ten million in killed alone. There is no doubt that war has sometimes been welcomed as a remedy for over-population. Thicknesse wrote in 1776: "A French gentleman told me above eight years since that France increased so rapidly in peace that they must necessarily have a war every twelve or fourteen years to carry off the *refuse* of the people". Many Germans have admitted their responsibility for the Great War, and justified it as "a biological necessity".

Other expedients, one or other of which has been almost universally adopted, are postponement of marriage—advocated by Malthus and operative both in the medieval village and now in the professional class; prolonged lactation or abstention from intercourse; infanticide; abortion; prevention of conception. The Greeks in their prolific period used to swarm periodically like bees, founding colonies everywhere from the Riviera to the Black Sea. Some Italian tribes did the same, under the name of *ver sacrum*. When the outlets for emigration were stopped, the Greeks resorted to female infanticide. It was rare for a Greek to rear more than one daughter. The male population was kept down by constant war and not infrequent massacre. In China the evidence is conclusive that female infanticide has till very lately been common, and both this and abortion were largely practised in Japan. Abortion is still far more common in civilised countries than is usually supposed. Miss Elderton has revealed the state of things in the north of England. Hirsch estimates that two million births are thus prevented annually in the United States, a number which seems to me incredible. A more recent estimate is 681,000, with 8,000 deaths. But in Berlin Burgdörfer says that there were more abortions than births in 1929, and the same was at one time true of Moscow, where cases were registered. In both countries the government has now taken energetic measures to stop the practice. As for the use of preventives, the commonest method, which is mentioned in the book of Genesis, has always been known. Chemical applications are mentioned by Soranus, whom St. Augustine calls *medicinae auctor nobilissimus*, in the third century.

It is difficult to say whether Christianity has favoured or discouraged fertility. On the one hand the Church condemned all irregular intercourse and tried more or less successfully to suppress, with the help of the criminal law, such evils as infanticide and abortion. On the other, it peopled the deserts with celibate hermits, founded thousands of monastic houses, and exalted virginity above marriage. To wield "the axe of virginity to cut down the wood of marriage" is an energetic phrase of St. Jerome. The Council of Trent anathematises those who say that virginity is not a higher state than marriage. In modern times the Roman Church sets its authority against all forms of birth-control, with a grudging concession to the use of the so-called safe period. In 1922 the Roman Catholic Archbishop of New York, after saying that "children troop down from heaven because God wills it", proceeds, "Even though some little angels in the flesh may appear to human eyes hideous, misshapen, a blot on civilised society, we must not lose sight of the Christian thought that under such visible malformation there lives an immortal soul to be saved". In the same year a preacher at Glasgow, after denouncing birth-control as "a crime calling for the punishments that befell Sodom and Gomorrah", suggests that if the world should ever become over-populated "the Lord may give another planet or create a new one for man to live on".

In the seventeenth and eighteenth centuries the prevailing view was that of Hume, that "the happiness of any society and its populousness are necessary attendants". There were, however, a few vigorous dissentients, among whom Arthur Young is conspicuous. Malthus never denied that his theories had been anticipated. The first edition of his famous book appeared in 1798; the second edition, virtually a new book, embodied the results of travels in several European countries; it was published in 1803.

According to Malthus, population tends to increase in a geometrical ratio, while food can only increase in an arithmetical ratio. Since this is untrue, the whole theory falls to the ground. It is, however, fair to say that Malthus disapproved of the practical application of his principle which has come to be associated with his name.

The agitation for birth-control was conducted mainly by Francis Place, but the two Mills, Grote, and others expressed approval. The movement seemed to have died down during the years when England was rich and prosperous; the famous trial of Bradlaugh and Mrs. Besant in 1876, which gave a world-wide advertisement to their propaganda, was well timed just before the depression which set in before 1880. The fall in the birth-rate began in England almost at once; our example was soon followed by most European countries. The cause, in my opinion, was not so much the diffusion of new knowledge as the suspension of the taboo which had made the very mention of the subject objectionable. When this taboo was once removed, the advantages of a small family were so numerous and cogent that there was very little scruple about taking advantage of the various methods which were known to avoid the birth of unwanted children.

Before coming to the main point of my lecture, which is to urge upon you that the decline in the birth-rate has reached such a level as to threaten the very existence of the civilised races, I wish to remove a few very common misconceptions. We are sometimes told that there must be a great many unmarried women because, in this country for example, there are two million more women than men. This is a fallacy. Nature, we may say, knowing that the female is the superior sex, has arranged that far more males shall be conceived than females. Miscarriages are generally of male embryos, but about 104 boys are born to 100 girls. At the procreative age, between twenty and forty, the numbers are practically equal, so that there is a Jack for every Jill, unless Jack gets killed in war. At all ages taken together there are more women, because women live three or four years longer than men.

The increase in population between 1760 and 1900 was quite phenomenal; there has never been anything like it, and never can be again, unless our Roman Catholic friend persuades the Almighty to "create a new planet". The cause of the increase was obviously the access to new and apparently almost unlimited supplies of food, which supported the masses whose labour was utilised by the "industrial revolution". It is often supposed that this increase was caused by a very high birth-rate. This again is untrue; the increase came about through a fall in the death-rate. For a long time the descending lines ran almost parallel; it is only lately that they have begun to draw together, since the death-rate, which has been halved in the last eighty years, cannot be reduced much further.

The confusion in the public mind on this subject is astonishing. On one side we hear people saying that the population is decreasing, which is not true, and on the other that since it is increasing there is nothing to be alarmed about. The crude rates are quite misleading, because they take no account of the ages of the population. Very young children and very old people have a high death-rate; where the large majority of the population is in the prime of life the crude death-rate will be low. The ages at which people are least likely to die are between eleven and fifteen. The result is that a country where the population is increasing rapidly will have a crude death-rate below the real death-rate; a country like France, where the numbers have been nearly stationary for a long time, will seem to be less healthy, by comparison with other countries, than it really is. The authorities give us a corrected table which in my opinion is almost as misleading as the crude rates. The only satisfactory method of computing the real death-rate of a country is to take the expectation of life at birth. There is a similar confusion about the birth-rate. People wonder at the very high birth-rate of countries like India, Palestine, and Egypt, and contrast their birth-rate of

50 with the meagre 15 of our own country. The books, so far as I know, neglect this point altogether. The reason for a birth-rate of 50 is that the large majority of the people are at the reproductive ages. In New Zealand, the healthiest country in the world, 75 per cent of the people reach the age of 60; in India only 14 per cent. The average number of children in an Indian family is not at all large.

It should therefore be easy to understand that a population may still be increasing though it is not replacing itself. This is the present condition of most of the European nations, the exceptions being chiefly among the Slavs, to whom it may be that the future belongs. The sixteen most rapidly growing populations in 1937 were Palestine, Syria, Dominican Republic, Uruguay, Argentina, Bolivia, Haiti, South Africa, Peru, Turkey, Puerto Rico, Mexico, Dutch East Indies, Siam, Salvador, Russia. The most densely populated countries are Belgium, England and Wales, Holland, Japan, Germany, Italy. India and China are saturated with population, and are not increasing rapidly.

Our country and Sweden have about the lowest birth-rates, lower even than France. The upper and middle classes are only half replacing themselves; the whole population only about two-thirds. Calculations have been made of the results in the future if the present decline goes on. "There is no assurance whatever," says Carr Saunders, "that children will come in numbers sufficient to prevent a decline of population and ultimate extinction." "If things remain as they are, the reproduction rate will fall, and the prospect will be a reduction of the population to less than a quarter of its present size a century from now."

The secretary of the Eugenics Society in 1936 prints a chart, based, as he says, on reasonable assumptions, showing that the birth-rate will fall from its present figure, 15, to 1.92 at the end of the century, while the death-rate will rise to 30.83. This is certainly near to "ultimate extinction".

The question arises whether this decline is altogether voluntary. The Italian expert, Professor Gini, believes that there is a cyclical rise and fall of reproductive vigour, and that "Western Europe is doomed". Professor Hankins of America, in a paper read at the 1931 Congress, without going so far as this, finds that the percentage of childless unions is six times as high in the United States as it was in the eighteenth century. Infertility seems to be very frequent among intellectual couples, most of whom would be glad to have children. "The disappearance of knightly and aristocratic houses in England and Germany is a striking illustration of the flux of population composition." But were these aristocrats so very intellectual? "Cultural evolution may be interfering with normal racial reproduction." This theory has not been proved, and I will express no opinion about it. But too "high" living certainly may interfere with fertility.

These are very gloomy forecasts; and what are we to do about it? For we cannot sit down and say that Western Europe is doomed, like Signor Gini. I do not believe in cycles, nor in analogies between the old age of individuals and the fate of nations. The writer whom I quoted just now will not have it that there is over-population, except in some congested areas, chiefly in the countries where rice is the staple food. Another writer says rather pertinently that if the world were over-populated we should expect to find agriculture prosperous, food expensive, and a lowered standard of living everywhere. Notoriously the opposite is what we have. No doubt there is an optimum population, but we cannot say what it is—such at least is the opinion of our English expert. Some however would say without hesitation that the highest average standard of living is the optimum.

Carr Saunders will not have it that unemployment is a sign that there are too many people in the country, and denies that emigration is a remedy. Only a few can be sent abroad, and their places are soon filled by new births. Besides, he does not want to send capable citizens out of the country, even to our own Dominions. He "cannot allow" a man with £800 a year to say that he would rather have a motor-car than a large family. The State must see to it that a man with several children is not handicapped as he is now. "It comes down to a matter of extending social services and allowances. This involves no revolution; it merely means an extension of existing services." Still, "a transformation of the whole scheme of life will have to be accomplished if the inconveniences attaching to parenthood are to be removed".

It is not to be supposed that the militaristic nations on the Continent have been slow to recognise the danger which threatens them hardly less than ourselves. And how have they tried to deal with it? All propaganda in favour of birth-control has been sternly forbidden. Every kind of influence in the power of the government has been brought to bear in favour of large families. Taxes have been imposed upon bachelors and childless persons. Substantial bonuses have been given to parents, with large presents, in some cases, to those who can show the fullest quivers. Nothing has been left undone to stimulate population. And what success have they had? In Italy the birth-rate has always been comparatively high, and under encouragement from the Government it is now just above unity —that is to say, the population of Italy is a little more than replenishing itself. The Nazi government also boasts of its success. The rate in Germany, which was only 14.7 when Hitler came into power, is now 19 or 20, again just above parity. But fifty years ago it was 36, and the very low number of 14 was due to the acute psychological discouragement which settled upon the country after the financial crisis of 1929. It is more than doubtful whether even this modest success can be maintained. The German Hausfrau, it seems, cannot be bribed or bullied into having more children than she wants. In France the failure of the campaign against family limitation is incontestable. The most that can be said of these counter-Malthusian crusades on the part of totalitarian governments is that without them the fall in the birth-rates would have been more rapid than it has been.

The failure in this propaganda invites certain reflections. We may reasonably congratulate ourselves on the proof that aggressive militarism is not omnipotent even in Germany. The average German and his wife will not incommode themselves in their home life in order to help the master race to conquer the world. The prospect of Germany finding *Lebensraum* for a swarming progeny by exterminating or deporting the inhabitants of neighbouring countries leaves them cold. This kind of ambition, the result of perverted romanticism, is out of date. But on the other hand what is happening on the Continent is rather ominous. No government has ever had so much power of indoctrinating its subjects or citizens with its own policy as these new dictatorships. No tyranny has ever been so searching, so ubiquitous. If they fail, they must be confronted with an almost invincible opposition. Even the Gestapo must remain outside the bedchamber of the married couple. We in this country neither have nor ever will have any means of coercing public opinion at all comparable to the methods of Hitler and Mussolini. If bribery and propaganda fail, what can we do?

Before trying to answer this question, I must say a few words on an objection which must have occurred to all of you. I have said nothing about the probable effects of this war upon population. I have not done so because the issue of the war is still doubtful, and still more because no one can foretell the possible sequelæ of the war in widespread revolution and civil war. The normal effects of a great war are to cause a rapid fall in the birth-rate while it is in progress, owing to the absence of husbands. In the Great War several millions of births were prevented in this way. In the year after the return of the soldiers there is a sharp rise above the normal rate. After this, the normal rate is resumed, but not entirely, since many potential fathers have been killed, and since the increase in certain diseases which are always more common in war-time is very prejudicial to fertility. A great war is always injurious both to the quantity and the quality of population; and I fear that the present world-wide conflagration will have permanent evil consequences. It is hardly an exaggeration to call it the suicide of European civilisation.

Well, then, in conclusion, what are we to do about it? In a free country there is only one thing to do—

to bring home to our people what is happening to
them. "There is a way which seemeth right unto a
man, but the end thereof are the ways of death." Is it
really conceivable that the peoples of Europe should
deliberately will or acquiesce in their own extinction?
There can never be another Europe. That contorted
peninsula of the great Asiatic land mass is the most
consummate piece of artistry, the masterpiece of the
Creator's skill. Land and water are so blended as to
produce the maximum of harmonious diversity in a
temperate and agreeable climate. Europe alone among
the continents has no deserts. Nowhere else can be
found so fine a branch of the human race as that
which has come into being as a blend of the Nordic,
Mediterranean, and Alpine stocks. Where else can
we find a civilisation so rich as that which combines
the legacies of Israel, Greece and Rome? Can anyone
maintain that Buddha and Confucius are better than
Christ and Plato? Is all this magnificent tradition to
be allowed to perish? Or take our own country, which,
like all continental writers, I call England, meaning,
of course, Great Britain. I am not going to please the
Scots by calling myself a Briton. I do not paint myself
blue, and I never offered a human sacrifice in my life.
Have we no legitimate pride in our country, the land
of Chaucer, Shakespeare, Milton, and Wordsworth,
of Newton and Darwin, of Nelson and Wellington? I
should think very poorly of anyone who was indifferent
to such an appeal. May we not also appeal to religion?
We know that some Christians call this world a vale
of tears, and wish that they had wings like a dove to
fly away from it. But this is rather cowardly. If "God
so loved the world that He gave His only Son to save
it", the world cannot be simply a place to run away

from. The modern Christian no longer expects the end of the world to come in his lifetime. He knows that we have probably an immensely long lease of our home. Do not some of us like to think that our own descendants may help to people the strange new world a hundred thousand years hence?

Let me beg of you, ladies and gentlemen, to do all in your power to counteract this fatal movement towards race suicide. All other social problems fade into insignificance compared with this. "To be or not to be, that is the question."

THE CHAIRMAN We shall all wish to thank the lecturer for his interesting though profoundly disquieting address. We shall none of us forget the earnest appeal with which he ended. But it is a good thing to hear both sides of a question. I see in the front row a gentleman who has been writhing with indignation and taking vicious notes. I think I will ask him to deliver his soul. It may be that he will be less pessimistic than the lecturer. At any rate a comparison of the two will give us something to think about.

THE HECKLER I do not want you to think that I disagree with all that the lecturer has said. Much of it I found very interesting. But I do disagree emphatically with his conclusions. Whenever we hear poor old Malthus abused, or when we are told that his theories are quite out of date, we always find either religious or political prejudice. The lecturer gave us some choice specimens of Roman Catholic teaching. We might have supposed that from motives of humanity Roman Catholics would have encouraged birth-control among Protestants, considering the awful fate which awaits them in the next world, unless they can plead "invincible ignorance". But they are beyond the reach of argument. The Whigs and Utilitarians supported Malthus from the first; the Tories and Radicals opposed him. Between these two opposites he became the best abused man of his time. When we consider that capitalists would naturally wish to see a redundancy of labourers competing for employment we might have expected radicals and socialists to welcome Malthus, who certainly wished well to the working class; but Marx and his followers were furious at a scheme of reform which by relieving misery would diminish class hatred. Even to this day many socialists dislike attempts to reduce the birth-rate. I must ask pardon for saying that some of the Council of the Eugenics Society are so carried away by their zeal for the political Left wing that they seem to forget that the original aim of the Society was to promote intrinsic improvement in the natural endowment of human beings. Malthus spoke of "positive checks", which he hoped to arrest by reducing fecundity. These were "unwholesome occupations, severe labour, extreme poverty, under-nourishment, and disease". He never said that food tends to increase at an arithmetical ratio, but that this ratio was the most that we had a right to expect. His main point was not the much criticised ratios, but that human fecundity, if un-checked, enormously exceeds the capacity of the earth to hold and maintain those who would be born, so that checks of one kind or another are essential. We have to choose the best. Of the truth of this there can be no doubt whatever.

The psychological basis of a positive population policy rests on the will to power. This may be dynastic, as in the days when war was the sport of kings, or nationalistic. Imperialism needs cannon-fodder.

Religious zeal makes people wish to increase the number of the faithful. There may be a cultural conviction that our own institutions are so good that they should be spread as widely as possible. Sheer megalomania is a common motive. Lastly, there is the mercantile wish for a reserve of labour, and for the largest possible number of purchasers. None of these motives appeal to the masses, who desire above all things a modicum of comfort, and security.

It is not true that we cannot say what the optimum population is. The standard of comfort is the test, and of course it fluctuates. As for the assertion that unemployment has nothing to do with over-population, it seems to me ridiculous. If there are one or two million idlers, who have to be supported out of the rates and taxes, the standard of living in the country is necessarily lowered by their presence. Equally absurd is the assertion that emigration brings no relief, and does not increase the population of the country which receives the immigrant.

Let us consider how we as a nation have behaved since the accident of our geographical position gave us for a time an advantage over our rivals on the Continent. The world acquiesced in our naval supremacy on two unwritten conditions. One was that we should keep our land army too small to be a danger to any continental power. That meant that we were not to engage in war on the Continent. The other was that we should throw open our ports to foreign trade, and not use our sea-power to injure the trade of any other nation. We were also not to keep aliens out of our colonies. We have chosen to violate these unwritten conditions just when our position was threatened. Then we applied the most violent prudential

173

stimulus to our population by allowing little children to earn wages. In order to pay for the food which this artificially created plethora required, we exported many millions of tons of our most irreplaceable source of wealth, coal, and thereby shortened the period of our commercial prosperity by at least a century. We also exported masses of machinery, to enable our rivals to dispense with our manufactures, and lent them vast sums of money, part of which may have been embezzled, but part was used in creating manufactures which would use the said machines. At the same time, the organisations of working men used their power to push up wages by political pressure beyond the economic level, and to shorten the hours of work. With a standard of living about thirty per cent above the most prosperous of our European rivals it is obvious that our home trade may flourish for a time, but that our export trade can be maintained only with extreme difficulty. Employers are further handicapped by an expenditure on "social services" which has no parallel in any other country.

The British workman has now not much survival value. No country welcomes him. Even in Canada notices are seen that "no British need apply". The following extract from Bruce Lockhart's *Guns or Butter* (1938) is as significant as it is disquieting. "Göteborg is the home town of the huge concern which supplies ball bearings to every country in the world. The company keeps very careful records of the respective efficiency of the workmen in the different nations. As production is standardised, the records afford a very fair standard of comparison. I was shown them. For the tiny ball bearings, which demand agile fingers, the French women come first. In the other categories the Swedes just beat the Americans. Very little behind come the Germans. And where do we come? I asked. The finger went down to the bottom. Easily last, said the manager. I'm afraid the British won't work or have forgotten how to."

We have forfeited our position as the workshop of the world. We are not willing to pay the price, and must take the consequences. The conditions which gave us a temporary advantage no longer exist. The huge population which those abnormal conditions brought into being is not an asset but a liability. They can no more live by exchanging their own products than a community can live by "taking in its other's washing". We depend for our existence on foreign trade, and our foreign trade is vanishing.

This is the state of things which our lecturer, following Professor Carr Saunders, proposes to remedy by throwing fresh burdens on the direct taxpayers, a minority of the nation already bled white by taxation. They are further insulted by being scolded for preferring a motor-car to a large family. It is as certain as anything can be that within one generation the upper and upper middle classes in England will be exterminated. I do not mean that they will be shot or guillotined; our methods are less violent but quite as effective. They will be exterminated in the sense that they will be financially ruined and no longer taxable. Then the working man will be in the position of a parasite which has killed its host. The wealth of the country will not be redistributed, it will have disappeared.

The gloomy prognostications about the extinction of our nation are in my opinion quite ridiculous. I should call it the fallacy of uncritical extrapolation. It is assumed that curves will continue in the same direction. In point of fact, the prediction has already been falsified, for the birth-rate rose instead of falling between 1933 and the outbreak of the war. What is happening is a quasi-automatic readjustment of equilibrium to meet changed conditions. I know that this readjustment is not consciously willed by individuals, but it is coming about just as the abnormal increase came about in the last century.

The lecturer said nothing about Raymond Pearl's "logistic curve", which predicts a gradual slowing down of the rate of increase, but nothing so catastrophic as the graphs on which the lecturer relies. Pearl's second curve corresponds fairly accurately with the facts hitherto observed, and several competent students of the subject have been convinced that Pearl has discovered a real law. I am rather sceptical myself, as many unpredictable events may disturb the calculation, and I do not see what is to happen when the asymptote is reached. Perhaps a downward curve of the same kind. I distrust all these extrapolations.

What we really have to expect is a reversion towards the England of the period before the industrial revolution. There will be improvements in agriculture. It is even possible that the American experiments in "dirtless farming" will introduce a revolution in the problem of food supply. But all improvements in technology reduce the number of manual labourers. We shall, I think, see an England with a population of about twenty millions, chiefly supported by home-grown food, with a moderate amount of foreign trade based on exchange of commodities. There is nothing to weep over in this termination of a wholly exceptional and not altogether desirable episode in our history. A gradual reduction of the population, spread over three generations, is the best way of tiding over the change without great suffering.

If the lecturer and his friends really want to increase the population, I will tell them how to set about it; certainly not by distributing what remains of the property of the minority in bribes to the majority. Let them begin by repealing the acts against child labour. This may restore the prudential stimulus of which I have spoken. Next, let them abolish the trade unions and institute competitive free labour. Then let them open our doors to Poles and Russians, or better still to Chinese and Japanese. Then, if there are still any countries which want to export food and import cheap manufactures, we may for a short time recover some of our foreign trade. The Argentine Republic might serve us for one generation; the other granaries of the world are filling up, and the manufacturing countries would raise their tariffs against us.

What I have said may sound like an indictment against my own countrymen. But other nations are in the same boat. Take the United States. We did not lose America in the reign of George the Third, but we are losing it now. The Anglo-Saxons in that country are a dwindling minority. In 1930 the "Foreign-born White Stock in New York State, according to Country of Origin," was thus classified. From North-Western Europe: Great Britain 221,145, Irish Free State 251,704, Scandinavia 123,522. From Central Europe: Poland 350,683, Germany 350,383, Austria 349,196, Hungary 70,631, Czechoslovakia 56,176. From Eastern Europe: Russia 481,306, Rumania 51,014, other countries 49,680. From Southern Europe, Italy 629,322, other countries 57,394. French Canadians and Mexicans, who are not excluded by quotas, are swarming into the country. The quota legislation has erected artificial barriers, and Asiatic immigration is almost entirely excluded, but it is plain that without interference the high-grade Americans of British origin would soon be completely swamped.

Or take the case of France. In 1931 the population of France was 41,834,923, of whom 2,891,168 were aliens, a proportion of 6.91. The actual facts were still worse, for very many aliens have been naturalised. The largest contingents of aliens come from Italy (easily first), Russia and Poland, Belgium and Spain. The French are leaving heavy manual work to foreigners. In mines, cement manufacture, chemical industries, public works, and sugar refining, from 41 to 47 per cent of the employees are aliens.

Civilisation, says Edward Carpenter, is a disease which nations catch. Most of them die of it. Both the Americans and the French think that they have a special gift for absorbing foreigners and imbuing them with their own qualities. We know that we have no such gifts, and perhaps it is as well that we do not welcome immigrants. Some ingredients in a melting-pot are not soluble. A far better remedy is that we should not be afraid of hard work.

I am afraid I have not been very civil to the lecturer, but the scare about depopulation annoys me very much. As he says himself, it is unthinkable that a nation like ours should will or consent to its own extinction.

THE CHAIRMAN Well, the two speakers have given us plenty to think about. I do not myself think that we shall commit suicide, but it is quite right that we should realise that the present surplus of births is deceptive, and that before long a decline, slow at first, may begin. The second speaker welcomes the prospect; we shall not all agree with him. In your name I thank them both.

II

SCENE: *The dining-table of Sir Duncan Mackenzie, M.D., F.R.S. Present—the host and Lady Mackenzie; Professor Clayton, a historian; the Dean of Barchester.*

LADY MACKENZIE Professor, I saw you at the Eugenics Lecture yesterday. What did you think of it?

CLAYTON I don't like scaremongers, and I think they are generally wrong. I should be ashamed to call myself either an optimist or a pessimist. An optimist is a barometer stuck at Set Fair, the kind of person who would buy from a Jew and sell to a Scot and expect to make a profit. The pessimist is stuck at Stormy; of two evils he chooses both. But I remember the old proverb that things will not be badly administered for long. Social institutions, like men and animals, generate anti-bodies to counteract toxins.

As I walked home after the lecture, four questions framed themselves in my mind. Does history show examples of nations which have adopted certain customs or habits under pressure, and have continued them, under changed conditions, to their own undoing? Is there any real analogy between the old age and death of an individual and that of a society? Is it a law that low-standard nations and classes displace those with a higher standard? Have there been physiological changes in the peoples of Europe which may partly account for the decline in their fertility?

The last question I hope will be answered by our host; the other three I will try to discuss, as briefly as possible.

There certainly have been cases where a nation has ruined itself by persisting in traditions which have become destructive. The history of the ancient Greeks is the most conspicuous instance. The Greeks, a very hardy and prolific race, were almost driven to civil war and infanticide when their outlets for emigration were closed, for the soil of Greece is very poor. It was a belief among them that before the Trojan war "the world was too full of people". The conquests of Alexander were followed by a great emigration to Asia, and some Asiatic Greeks became rich, but we do not know what proportion of the European Greeks migrated. The Romans drained their eastern provinces of their prosperity, and the backwash of Orientalism at last submerged the Greek element in the former Seleucid empire. Greece was already half empty in the time of Polybius, in consequence of race-suicide, he thinks, and in the Dark Ages successive waves of invaders almost obliterated the Hellenic stock. We may say that the ancient Greeks, the most highly endowed race that ever existed, have disappeared from history, though in South Italy, Sicily, and some of the islands one may see some typically Greek faces.

The ancient Romans also became virtually extinct. The causes of the decline and fall of Rome are a well-known and fascinating problem. Countless books have been written about it, and perhaps all the known causes together hardly explain the extent of the catastrophe. One has to take account of the unproductive rapacity of the Capital, of the ruinous results of slavery, of the massacres of the old families by the emperors, of the prevalence of vicious celibacy, of the dishonesty of the Roman mint (inflation we call it now) which destroyed the middle class, of the chaos and devastations in the third century, of epidemics and possibly of malaria. Even this enumeration is not exhaustive. The Empire was still well peopled under the Antonines, though I do not accept Tertullian's rhetorical statements as true of the whole Empire. There was probably a heavy fall in the third century, which was never retrieved. The death-rate, so far as scholars have computed from inscriptions, was high, but not very high. The expectation of life at birth was about twenty-five years, about the same as in Western Europe before the eighteenth century. But of course the death-rate of the slave population may have been much higher, and their birth-rate very low. It is certainly significant that in a people where family pride was inordinately strong the obscure clan of the Anicii alone survived, to be treated with as much deference as the Howards or Percys. The excellent portraits, of which there are many, show that the typical Roman face, powerful and bull-necked, had disappeared.

Other examples of depopulation and race-suicide are less important for our present purpose. The inhabitants of the Greater Antilles disappeared under Spanish oppression; so did the Guanches of the Canary Islands. The last Tasmanian is dead. Stevenson gives a graphic description of the approaching extinction of the Marquesas islanders, among whom hardly any children are born. He thinks that the South Pacific islands were once over-populated, and that restriction, once adopted almost from necessity, has been continued till the race is doomed, in some of the islands though not in all.

Is there any parallel between the decay of the Greeks and Romans and the present situation in Europe? On the whole I do not think so. A world full of slaves and empty of machines cannot be compared with modern Europe. Besides the immense and obvious differences between ancient and modern civilisation, the causes which made these two great nations withdraw from the struggle for existence were largely psychological. All through antiquity there was an undercurrent of pessimism or pejorism. There was hardly any belief in progress, and a general opinion that the golden age, if there was one, was in the past, not in the future. We find melancholy reflections even in the classical age of Greek literature. Sophocles anticipates Bacon's lines, "What then remains but that we still should cry Not to be born, or being born to die". Even at the height of Roman power Lucretius and Horace lament the degeneracy of the age. In the third century and after, a chorus of woe resounds from all sides. Pessimism almost swamped the buoyant ship of Christianity. "The world is at its last gasp," said Julian the emperor. Now when people have given up hopes of human society, when life seems to them to be not worth living, they always seek and find compensation in some religion or philosophy of escape. Philosophy may teach them that there is an "intelligible world" behind earth's vain shadows. Religion may teach them that there is a future life in which the injustices and miseries of this life are redressed.

In one way or another, as Canning said rather too hopefully of the Dago republics, they call a new world into existence to redress the balance of the old.

But there is hardly a trace of this escapism in our modern society, unless we give that name to the apocalyptic visions of the socialists, which have faded a good deal lately. Besides, hopes for a good time coming would not depress the birth-rate. No, I do not think there is anything in this analogy. We no longer believe in human perfectibility; we no longer look at the future through the rose-coloured spectacles of Lord Macaulay. But as for thinking that it is cruel to bring children into such a world as this is going to be, I see no signs of such a feeling. My conclusion is that though under certain conditions a nation may withdraw from the battle and seek repose in Nirvana, those conditions are not present in Europe to-day.

My second question was whether nations, or phases of civilisation, grow old and die. This seems to be the thesis of Spengler's famous book on the Decline of the West. History passes through cycles. Culture degenerates into civilisation, and then into a state which is no longer interesting to a historian. But I can see no reason why a civilisation should pass into senile decay. The germ-plasm does not grow old; the hen, as Samuel Butler says, is only a device to preserve the egg. The strong point of the theory is not biological. Civilisations do seem to have flourished for a time and then decayed. But in every case there seems to be some ascertainable cause—foreign conquest, a change in trade routes, dysgenic reproduction, exhaustion of the soil, or the *taedium vitae* which we have refused to regard as inevitable. No doubt there is something in Aristotle's theory that every art, and every institution, advances till it reaches its *telos*, its full development, and then "stops". Perhaps the free Greek States and the Roman *res publica* produced all the fruits that they could. But

I do not think there is any biological law which need make us think that western civilisation is doomed.

My third question. Is there a law that nations with a low standard of living must displace those with a higher standard, and that for the same reason the richer classes must make way for the poorer? Here I am sorry to say that I agree with the second speaker at the Eugenics meeting. He showed us how cheap labour is ousting dear labour in France and the United States. The Americans have had to stop or check the immigration of cheap labour; but Maine is full of French Canadians, who have taken possession of derelict farms and villages, and there are a million and a half Mexicans in the Southern States, though they are not regarded as very desirable citizens. The ascendancy of the white man began with three famous voyages. When Columbus, on his way, as he thought, to the East Indies, struck the Bahama Islands; when in 1494 Vasco da Gama rounded the Cape of Good Hope; and when Magellan reached the Philippines from Patagonia, the long blockade of Europe by the Asiatics was broken. By a stroke of good fortune which can never be repeated, the European was able to occupy and partially populate three vast and almost empty continents, the two Americas and Australasia. The Russians made equally spectacular conquests in northern Asia, and nearly the whole of Africa was staked out for European exploitation. In 1914, out of 53 million square miles—the habitable surface of the globe—only six millions were not under the rule of the white races. But the tide had already begun to turn. The defeat of Russia by Japan sent a thrill of hope through Asia; the murderous civil wars of the European nations have made them think that their time is soon coming. The Japanese Count Okuma, who in 1907 had exclaimed "Let us go to India, where the people are looking for our help", wrote in 1919, "By marching westward to the Balkans, to Germany, France, and Italy, the greater part of the world may be brought under our sway". Another Japanese writes in 1916: "How our strength grows! In 1895 we conquered China; Russia, Germany and France stole the booty from us. In ten years we punished Russia and took back our own; in twenty we were quits with Germany; with France there was no need for haste. As for America, that fatuous booby with much money and no brains, she is an immense melon, ripe for the cutting. North America will support a thousand million people; they shall be Japanese and their slaves." We laughed at them, and put the Mikado on the comic stage.

The Americans, Canadians and Australians are under no illusions about the yellow man. "Nowhere, absolutely nowhere, can white labour compete with coloured labour." The white labourer lives on sufferance behind a "Chinese wall" of battleships and bayonets. The yellow man is excluded solely by force. Once let him break through the cordon, and in a few years there would be no white men left. Such at least is the unanimous opinion of those who are threatened in any way by Asiatic immigration. We may remember the excitement of the Labour Party at home about Chinese labour on the Rand. The hypocritical anxiety about the morals of the labourers did not conceal the real reason—that the Chinaman gives much better value for his wages than the Englishman.

I may be reminded that countries where the standard of living is very low are miserably poor, and that there is no trade because nobody can afford to buy. It is true that a high standard may be maintained where a country is self-sufficing, where the population does not exceed the production of food, and where the people are industrious and intelligent. But a nation which depends for its existence on foreign trade can never be a working man's paradise. The American doctrine of "consumptionism" means in practice that people are to be induced by the arts of salesmanship to buy things that they do not want or ought not to want. It means intolerable wastefulness and an artificial multiplication of wants. Such a civilisation is in a very precarious position when confronted with Asiatic competition.

We are not doomed, because we may if we choose reduce our wants, work harder, and live in rather hard training. We are doing it now, and it does not hurt us much.

DEAN OF BARCHESTER I agree, and I think all Christians ought to advocate this course. "Thou therefore endure hardship, as a good soldier of Jesus Christ." To live in hard training—that is all that "asceticism" means. Plain living and high thinking.

MACKENZIE As a physician I say ditto to the Professor and the Dean. We want to simplify our lives, which are now lived in a state of unnecessary nervous strain.

CLAYTON Of course the example must be given by those at the top.

MACKENZIE I think it is being given. The possessing classes have completely altered their way of living without squealing at all. That gives me some little hope for the future, if only our professional mischief-makers would let the working man alone.

CLAYTON Well, I have answered my three questions as well as I could in a few minutes. Now for my fourth. Is the fall in the birth-rate partly involuntary and due to a physiological change? This is a question for you, Sir Duncan.

MACKENZIE That is a very difficult question to answer. It is often supposed that the reproductive urge is stronger among savages than among civilised peoples. The opposite is the truth. The reason why fertility rites among savages are sometimes so unpleasant is that it takes more to excite a savage than a civilised man. Some savage tribes are licentious, but that is not true of primitive races generally. On the other hand, there is the well-known problem of differential class-fertility. The richer and better educated classes almost everywhere have smaller families. But on this subject there are two things that ought to be remembered; I do not think they were mentioned at the lecture, but I was not there. One is that the upper classes marry later. The artisan may be earning his full wages at twenty-five; the professional man is usually very badly paid at first, and sometimes, it may be thought, over-paid later. The other is that if wealth and small families are associated, that may be partly because money tends to accumulate in small families. Galton thought that one reason why aristocratic families often die out is that the young aristocrat likes to marry an heiress, "the last representative of a dwindling family," who is very often barren. But I must say that my experience, and that of many other doctors, is that in the upper classes there are many more sterile marriages than among the poor, and that the number tends to increase. Many women in these classes are unable to suckle their infants. Raymond Pearl has proved that among brain-workers married couples come together much less often than those who labour in the open air, and this may have something to do with the lower fertility of the former. I have no doubt at all that many childless couples would like to have children; we are often consulted on this subject by husband or wife or both.

Is it likely that a great physiological change has come about in so short a time as fifty years, for this is what we have to consider? I do not think it at all impossible, when I examine the extraordinary changes in the causes of death which have taken place in the same period. I do not know whether you will care to look at these tables. Those of my medical brethren to whom I have shown them have been much interested and a good deal surprised. The American statistics were drawn up for the Metropolitan Life Insurance Company; the table for England and Wales in the year 1933 was compiled by myself. Of the American tables, the first column is for 1901-4, the second for 1925-9. They both give the twenty commonest causes of death. Not only has the order changed greatly, but only eleven out of twenty occur in both lists. In order of frequency these are the lists.

United States 1901-4	United States 1925-9	England and Wales 1933
1 Tuberculosis	1 Heart disease	1 Heart disease
2 Pneumonia	2 Cancer	2 Cancer
3 Heart disease	3 Pneumonia	3 Tuberculosis
4 Nephritis	4 Nephritis	4 Pneumonia
5 Diarrhœa	5 Apoplexy	5 Apoplexy
6 Apoplexy	6 Tuberculosis	6 Influenza
7 Cancer	7 Premature birth	7 Arteriosclerosis
8 Ill-defined causes	8 Influenza	8 Bronchitis
9 Old age	9 Diabetes	9 Old age
10 Bronchitis	10 Auto. accidents	10 Nephritis
11 Meningitis	11 Angina pectoris	11 Rheumatism
12 Diphtheria	12 Diarrhœa	12 Auto. accidents, etc.

United States 1901-4	United States 1925-9	England and Wales 1933
13 Premature birth	13 Accidental falls	13 Premature birth
14 Typhoid	14 Appendicitis	14 Diabetes
15 Influenza	15 Suicide	15 Suicide
16 Paralysis	16 Congenital malformation	16 Diarrhœa
17 Congenital debility	17 Puerperal state	17 Gastric ulcer
18 Convulsions	18 Hernia	18 Prostate
19 Other diseases of stomach	19 Bronchitis	19 Appendicitis
20 Lack of care	20 Diphtheria	

A comparison between the most prevalent fatal diseases in England and America does not call for much comment. Bronchitis is more deadly in England, nephritis in America. The disappearance of old age in the second American table reminds us that in America the saving of life has been almost entirely at the ages before 50.

The changes in a quarter of a century have been very remarkable. There has been a real increase in heart disease and cancer, but not quite so great as the figures suggest. Our young practitioners will not let their patients die of "old age" if they can help it. They must give some better excuse. But there is one affection of the heart, coronary thrombosis (it appears in the second American list as angina pectoris), which has increased about sixfold in twenty years; I cannot tell why. Other diseases have increased rapidly in both countries—diabetes for instance.

CLAYTON I thought insulin had deprived that disease of its terrors.

MACKENZIE No. Insulin prolongs the life of the diabetic on an average eight or ten years, but it is no cure. If we want to reduce the cases of diabetes we must put everybody on strict rations. There was a heavy fall, brought about in this way, during the Great War.

CLAYTON   But do people overeat more than they used to?

MACKENZIE   The rich eat less, much less, but the poor eat more.

DEAN OF BARCHESTER   Sir Duncan, there are one or two questions that I want to ask you. You know that poor Malthus, who was really very orthodox in his opinions, recommended later marriages as the remedy for over-population. Our young people have read Freud, or more often have not read him, and they have been told that repression is very bad for the health, and that, as someone has said, outraged Nature has her revenges. They talk to us parsons sometimes, but they think that we do not tell them the truth. I want to tell them the truth, but I am not quite sure what the truth is. For instance, many years ago I was dining with a housemaster at Eton. A boy in his house very nearly died of pleurisy. His father came down, and a leading London doctor. As soon as the boy was out of danger, the father, a nasty-minded old colonel, began to enjoy himself. "I say, doctor," he said, "I suppose you could have cured a good many of your female patients by a remedy which you did not dare to prescribe?" The doctor shrugged his shoulders and said, "Scores": I am not sure that he did not say "Hundreds". What is the truth about that?

MACKENZIE   Speaking merely as a physician, I should say that every girl ought to have a baby at twenty-one.

LADY MACKENZIE   Really, Duncan!

MACKENZIE   I don't tell them so, of course.

DEAN OF BARCHESTER Well, hardly! But as regards men, do not you sometimes have patients who complain that they are pestered, and who expect you to give them leave to find relief with what Lucretius calls Venus volgivaga?

MACKENZIE That is advice which I have never given and never will give. I have never known a case of serious illness caused by repression.

DEAN OF BARCHESTER But unhappiness and mental disturbance?

MACKENZIE Yes, minor neuroses, not infrequently, but chiefly, I think, with neurotic persons who make no effort to control their thoughts. The average healthy man does not suffer by living strictly. But I admit there are exceptions.

DEAN OF BARCHESTER Long ago I was consulted by a very able young fellow, about thirty, who was doing very well in his profession. He told me that he had lately, for the first time, been much troubled by obsessions of this kind. I gave him the advice which we always give in such cases, and told him that I could not guarantee success. If he could not get rid of the trouble, I advised him to marry. As I half suspected, he told me that he was in love, but he thought that as a gentleman he ought not to ask a nice girl to marry him until he had conquered this humiliating temptation. I said, My dear fellow, go and ask her at once. That case of mine ended very happily.

MACKENZIE You did quite right; I have had very similar cases.

DEAN OF BARCHESTER Thank you, Sir Duncan. But now I want to unburden my mind about this whole subject. Only, Lady Mackenzie, if I do, I shall have to touch upon some unpleasant things. Perhaps I had better wait till you leave the dining-room.

LADY MACKENZIE Please speak quite freely, Mr. Dean. This is a woman's question quite as much as a man's, and I am a doctor's wife.

DEAN OF BARCHESTER I have never taken part in the agitation against birth-control, because it is surely obvious that we cannot have both the old birth-rate and the new death-rate. In three generations the death-rate has fallen from 22 to 11. But I sometimes think that this is not an isolated question, but a small part of the greatest moral rebellion in history, and this really frightens me. The opponents of birth-control used very bad arguments and sometimes made themselves ridiculous; but they felt in their bones that the whole foundations of traditional morality were being undermined, and that the arguments used to justify birth-restriction might also be employed to destroy all the safeguards which long experience has erected against a ruinous disregard of all moral sanctions. Birth-control has now been accepted as a necessity; but it is not uncommon even now to meet people who regard it with moral indignation and disgust, mainly, I think, because they feel that the barriers against far more objectionable practices have been thrown down, and they do not see any logical halting-place. The Roman Church is always guided by the prudence which comes of long experience of human nature. It refuses to be carried away by winds of doctrine; the winds change, but human nature remains the same.

What a change there has been about adultery and divorce! Some people seem to have a vague idea that the seventh commandment was invented by Queen

Victoria. Smart society seems to have gone back to the morals of the Regency. Look at Burke's Peerage. On every few pages we read "marriage dissolved by divorce"; there is no shame about it. One might have supposed that the deliberate breach of the most solemn contract ever entered upon by man and woman was a highly disgraceful act, and that to break up a friend's home was the act of a champion cad, which ought to exclude offenders of both sexes from decent society. But divorced couples, whitewashed by a subsequent marriage, are by no means social outcasts. In 1913 there were 827 divorces in Great Britain; in 1936 there were 4,699. Things are no better in other countries; in the United States they are even worse.

Has there been an increase in pre-nuptial unchastity? Prostitution has happily diminished; in its coarser forms it is not only cruel but disgusting. American investigators report that the men are becoming more virtuous, the women less so. Dr. Hamilton of New York obtained answers from a hundred men and a hundred women in New York. Fifty-nine men and forty-seven women had committed acts of immorality with other persons before marriage. I confess that the large number of unchaste women was a shock to me. I fear there is no doubt that access to contraceptives has greatly increased this kind of irregularity.

Another unpleasant symptom is the rapid increase in homosexual offences. In 1910 to 1914 the annual number of convictions was 307; in 1936 it was 1,167. The facts are probably worse, for to avoid scandal the offender is often warned that a warrant has been issued for his arrest, and the wretch is allowed twenty-four hours to make his escape from the country. We most of us know of distinguished public men, and, alas, of clergymen, whose careers have been blasted in this way. In Germany there has been a regular cult of the vice. Numerous *Nachtlokals* are, or were, devoted to it. Under the Weimar republic there was open solicitation in the streets and at the doors of hotels. In many countries an offence which was formerly punished with death is not punished at all, unless young boys are concerned. And yet not so long ago the crime was unmentionable, "not to be named among Christians". I am told (I have not verified the story) that in the London Museum there is a newspaper report of a trial for this offence in the early part of the last century. The judge in sentencing the prisoners informed them that they had endangered the lives of their fellow-citizens, for it was quite possible that the Almighty would be provoked into destroying London, like Sodom, by incendiary bombs. The culprits were to be hanged separately, so that their presence might not contaminate any murderers or highwaymen who had been sent to execution on the same day. We must again admit that the change in public opinion has been enormous.

The same applies to bestiality and incest. The former, we are told, does nobody any harm and ought not to be a crime. The latter is considered undesirable, on ludicrously inadequate grounds. We think of a famous passage of Plato, a "poor benighted heathen", and wonder what has happened to us.

MACKENZIE   One moment, Mr. Dean. Let me fetch my Jowett, and we will read that passage. It will take the bad taste out of our mouths. It is in the *Laws*, I think; vol. five.

DEAN OF BARCHESTER   Thank you. This is what Plato

says: "There is another matter of great importance
and difficulty, concerning which God should legislate
if there were any possibility of obtaining from him an
ordinance about it. But seeing that divine aid is not
to be had, there appears to be a need of some bold
man who specially honours plainness of speech, and
will say outright what he thinks best for the city and
citizens. . . . How will our young men and maidens
abstain from desires which thrust many a man and
woman into perdition, and from which reason,
assuming the functions of law, commands them to
abstain? . . . Upon reflection I see a way of imposing
the law, which in one respect is easy, but in another
very difficult. We all know that most men, in spite of
their lawless natures, are sometimes very strictly
restrained from intercourse with the fair, and entirely
with their own will. When do you mean? asks the
other. When anyone has a brother or a sister who is
fair, nothing unseemly ever takes place between them,
nor does the thought of such a thing ever enter the
minds of most of them. Does not a little word extinguish all pleasures of that sort? What word? The
declaration that they are unholy, hated of God, and
most infamous, and is not the reason of this that
everyone from his childhood has heard men speaking
in this same manner about them, always and everywhere? . . . The legislator then will consecrate the
tradition of their evil character among all, and that
will be the surest foundation of the law which he can
make. . . . Such a law, extending to other sensual
desires and conquering them, would be the source of
innumerable blessings. . . . I can imagine some lusty
youth who is standing by, and who on hearing this
enactment declares in scurrilous terms that we are

making foolish and impossible laws, and fills the world with his outcry. . . . But have we not heard of Iccus of Tarentum, who with a view to the Olympic and other contests, in his zeal for his art, and because he was of a manly and temperate disposition, lived chastely during the whole time of his training? The same is said of many others; and yet they were far worse educated in their minds than your and my citizens, and in their bodies far more lusty. . . . And had they the courage to abstain from what is deemed a pleasure for the sake of a victory in wrestling, running, and the like; and shall our young men be incapable of a similar endurance for the sake of a much nobler victory, which is the noblest of all, as from their youth we will tell them, the victory over pleasure, which if they win they will live happily, or if they are conquered the reverse of happily." I wonder whether St. Paul had seen this passage. Probably not, but he repeats it almost word for word.

Plato was too fond of making laws, like a Fascist dictator. That we all admit; but may we not learn from him three important truths? First, the great importance of keeping up sound traditions. Second, that the true harmony is not a harmony of satisfied impulses—there is no harmony on that road—but a harmony of conscious purposes, to be won by unending self-discipline. And thirdly, that some things are wrong not because they hurt anyone but because they are an offence against the law of God written in our hearts. If this law condemns some actions as infamous, it is useless to ask why they are infamous; they are so, and there is an end of it.

How far is this "Why shouldn't I" to go? How about artificial insemination, with what necessarily precedes

196

it? This is being done already, with increasing frequency and increasing success. We come at last to
Aldous Huxley's *Brave New World*, a horrible book
with a very honest purpose. The same author, in his
Ends and Means, is quite puritanical. Do you see what
troubles me? Where are we to draw the line? If we
go all the way with these bold despisers of taboos, all
moralists from Plato downwards, and of course all
Christian teachers, have been absolutely wrong. That
is a large pill to swallow.

CLAYTON There is a great deal of truth in your
indictment. But as a historian I don't believe in big
sudden changes. Periods of licence and of Puritanism
seem to alternate. Nevertheless, we are in the middle
of a terrible earthquake, and strange things may
happen.

LADY MACKENZIE Mr. Dean, have faith in us
women. We are the guardians of tradition, and now
that we are citizens we will not allow the men to go
too far off the rails.

CLAYTON I have a great faith in sound feminine
instinct. And yet I remember an Oxford don saying
that no woman knows the difference between *phusis*
and *nomos*.

LADY MACKENZIE I know what that means. *Phusis*
is the law of nature, *nomos* is convention or tradition.
That is just the sort of thing that a don would say.
We honour tradition because we know that it is
founded on nature. Tradition is not infallible, but it is
never wholly negligible. That is what our young hot-
heads forget. Their plants have no roots and will soon
wither.